AMELS
AMELING
AMELISTS

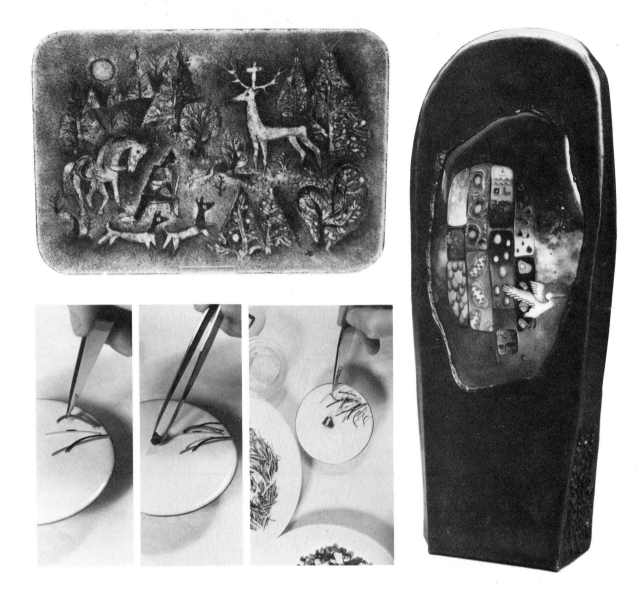

Glenice Lesley Matthews

Photographs by MICHAEL J. OLIVER *unless otherwise noted*
HAROLD B. HELWIG, *technical consultant*

CHILTON BOOK COMPANY   *Radnor, Pennsylvania*

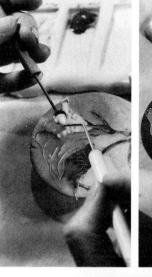

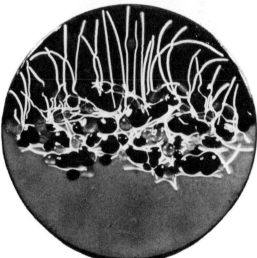

ENAMELS
ENAMELING
ENAMELISTS

Designed by Adrianne Onderdonk Dudden
Manufactured in the United States of America

Library of Congress Cataloging in Publication Data
Matthews, Glenice Lesley.
    Enamels, enameling, enamelists.
    Includes index.
    1. Enamel and enameling—Technique.   I. Title.
NK5000.M36   1984   738.4   83-70776
ISBN 0-8019-7285-X

Front panel: *Three Swans*, Triptych bracelet #10. Colette.
Cloisonné enamel; gold, silver, gems. Photograph, the artist.

Figures on Title Page Spread, reading across both pages clockwise
from top left corner (see specific pages for full captions and
details of work): Karl Drerup, artist, page 6; Colette, artist,
page 4; David C. Freda, artist, page 14; cloisonné sequence,
pages 107–108; Pamela Carey Steele, artist, page 14; enameling
supplies; threads and blobs sequence, pages 80–81.

The author and publisher assume no responsibility and hereby disclaim
all liability for injuries or damage resulting from the use or misuse
of equipment and/or materials described in this book.
Appropriate safety precautions are described
in detail and must be followed to the letter when using lead-bearing
enamels or acids, or when operating a kiln.

1 2 3 4 5 6 7 8 9 0   2 1 0 9 8 7 6 5 4

For T, who from an early age guided my growth
and understanding of the fantasies
of this world through patience and humility.

Contents

Foreword

Most of the many books which have been written about enameling over the past forty years are out of print. The author's sincerity in each book varied, dependent on his or her attitude toward the student in juxtaposition to the author's own abilities and ego. Few were good, many were adequate and most forgot about the student confidence necessary when beginning this versatile medium by going too far too quickly or by circumventing fundamental technology with technique.

The principal objective of this book is to open attitudes and build confidence while solving the difficulties present while working with tools and materials in unfamiliar processes. The repeating instructions for basic procedures makes the text elementary in presentation. However, learning is the practice of perfecting skills, as well as reinforcing knowledge. The book's methods are based on the practical experience of teaching and learning at the same time. Thus, the attitude expressed herein makes this a clear guide for anyone desiring to learn the rudiments of enameling.

The inexperienced enamelist will be greatly encouraged in how to secure good results with this reliable information. However far the information is taken, not all questions will be removed. One has to have obtained enough work and thought encounters to be able both to formulate questions and to understand answers.

Preparing a succinct account of enameling for the novice is not an easy task. Long-term enamelists tend to forget just how difficult it was to become cognizant of the processes. Elemental simplicities were assimilated over a period of time through combined knowledge and repetitive practice. Such subtleties are unknown to the naive and overlooked in practiced detail by the theorist. The contents of this first-approach text captures the midstream logic of how each step develops, defines and influences the results. This is done with neither a heavy hand nor in a light-hearted manner, but with open-ended guidance, clearly stated. The procedures and projects are easily accomplished, preparing one to strive toward higher goals when doing one's own personal work.

The overall value of how-to books, although always questionable in my mind, is of interest only if the audience addressed is presented with complete, unique and well-grounded direction pertaining to success, rather than wasted time. The most important factor is that the contents allow the participant to change procedures after the processes are learned without fear or guilt of taking charge of their own work habits. It is the responsibility of the maker to bring value to the work, not the book's or the author's. The statement or art of the piece is derived from only one source: the person actually doing the work.

Portions from traditional, classical and contemporary enameling technology are fundamentally blended as process with reason rather than rhyme. This book contains a whole beginning, not to design, but to enamel. Every paragraph, photograph or phrase can be understood. All is, and in, relationship. Health hazards as well as the individual applications of an enamel are treated with equal importance and must be noted in context. Glenice Matthews has established understandable partnerships between the reader, author, teacher, student, idea, process, material and the act of enameling on metal. The practical knowledge presented is systematic, polite and considered, bringing the enamelist to simple victories and successful beginnings.

Harold B. Helwig

Acknowledgments

Many special people contributed their skills, support, technical knowledge, and examples of their fine enamels to make this book possible. Although it would be impossible to name all contributors, I wish to express heartfelt thanks to: Michael J. Oliver, who had to share his life with this book on a daily basis and whose photographic skills I could not have been without; the positive technical and aesthetic assistance of Bill Helwig; Patricia Cadden, for the original idea; Lynn Seydel, my diligent typist; The Wichita Art Association enameling class, especially Kay Johnson, Marydelight Mylar, and Bertie Wilson, whose helping hands were always ready; The Ceramic Coating Company for their technical services; Seaire Manufacturing for kiln furniture and supplies; the Spring Street Enamels Gallery; every fine enamelist who supported my requests and responded with enthusiasm; and my editor and staff, who coordinated everything to become a whole. These few, and many other wonderful people help enameling perpetuate its fascination. Thank you.

May Hephaestus keep your fires burning and your hand true.

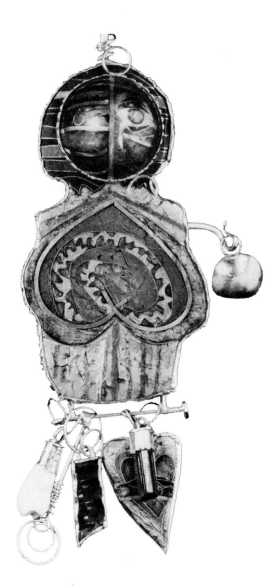

The basics

Fig. 1-1 Along the Payette, 1982. *John Killmaster. Limoges/silkscreen enamels on steel panel; 14″ × 22″. Photograph, H. Huff.*

·1·
An introduction to enameling

This book is intended to function at many levels. The experienced enamelist, the inexperienced enamelist, instructors of enameling, and the interested layperson will all find merit within these covers and enamelists will consider this text "how one can enamel," rather than "how to enamel."

Part One introduces the materials and processes, covers safety precautions and equipment, basic firing procedures, and the preparation of enamels and metal base materials for use. In brief, everything you need to know *before* you begin to enamel.

The six projects in Part Two are designed to introduce the enamelist to a variety of techniques and to give basic, step-by-step instructions that will enable even the newcomer to enamel successfully. Part Three provides information for finishing and mounting, problem-solving, and alternative methods of enamel application. Descriptions and examples of 26 enameling techniques are provided in Part Four.

But first, a short history of enameling.

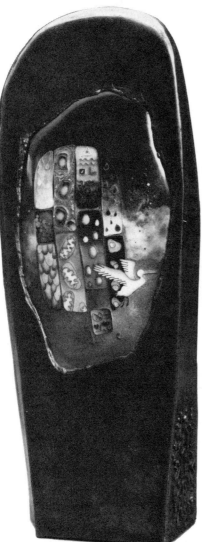

Fig. 1-2 Column #3 with Cellular Form and Pelican, *Aperture Series. Colette. Enamel on fine silver; 24K gold cloisonné wire; electroformed copper; $7\frac{1}{2}'' \times 3\frac{1}{4}'' \times 3''$. Photograph, the artist.*

Fig. 1-3 Little Sea Treasure Chest. *Marlene Byer. Limoges enamel on electroplated copper, silver foil; $2\frac{3}{4}''$ cube. Courtesy of Spring Street Enamels Gallery.*

Fig. 1-4 Blue Rose, *1980. Kathryn Regier Gough. Fine silver cloisonné; 8mm Biwa pearls; $2\frac{1}{2}$" × 2". Photograph, the artist.*

What is enameling? A brief history

Enameling, the process of applying small granules of enamel to metal and firing at high temperatures, is simply glass on metal. Ever since man discovered fire and found that silica turned to glass when heated to extreme temperatures, there has been some form of glass on metal. Throughout history, man has decorated his body and his belongings to make them more beautiful, more individual. Anthropological examples of decorative glass and metal objects have been found. The hypothesis of when and how glass and metal were combined to become a decorative enamel as we know it today still remains the conjecture of many art historians.

For our viewing pleasure in art museums throughout the world, examples of the early craftsman's art is displayed: Egyptian, Greek,

Fig. 1-5 Weight sculpture. James Malenda. Enamels on copper, nickel, silver, wood, paint; 24" × 12" × 6". Courtesy of Spring Street Enamels Gallery.*

Fig. 1-6 Eustace, 1949. Karl Dre-
rup. Opaque enamels; $10\frac{1}{4}''\times7\frac{1}{4}''$.
In the collection of The Wichita Art
Association, Inc.

Fig. 1-7 Cross, 1960. Charles
Bartley Jeffery. Concave cloisonné
and ebony cross; $3\frac{1}{2}''\times2''$. In the
collection of The Wichita Art Association, Inc.

Fig. 1-8 Stop and Go, *1953. Arthur Ames. Enamels on copper; 8¾". In the collection of The Wichita Art Association, Inc.*

Fig. 1-9 Madonna, *1952. Jean Ames. Enamels on copper; 8¾" diameter. In the collection of The Wichita Art Association, Inc.*

Celt, Chinese, Japanese. The enamel tradition continues throughout the ages with examples from the Byzantine, Renaissaince Italy, Limoges, France, Russia, and 18th-Century England. The mystical lusciousness of an enamel surface has fascinated the goldsmith of many ages and cultures. The seductive quality of precious metal reflecting through a crystal-clear colorful transparent enamel, or the subtlety of opaque enamels, has kept the artisan spellbound for centuries.

In the United States of America, this century has produced its own flowering of the enamelist's art. Louis Tiffany, working in New York at the turn of the century, produced limited edition and individual enamels for clients (see color section). Rare now, they still can be found by the serious collector. Although enameling once flourished in industry as a durable finish for metal products, the artist-craftsman's pursuit of this medium has risen and fallen according to current popularity.

Kenneth Bates is considered to be the Dean of American enamelists. His diligence and perseverance have paved the way for all serious enamelists to follow. His devotion to enameling and his artistic standards have elevated enameling to a serious artform (see color section for an example of Bates's work). Enameling is now part of the art curriculum in many schools, universities and art schools. The Cleveland Art Institute is one example of an institution that has fostered the art of enameling.

During the latter part of the Twentieth Century, numerous artists have presented their own interpretations of the enameling arts and should be recognized for their outstanding contribution. These pioneers of enameling paved the way for today's contemporaries.

Fig. 1-10 Am I My Brother's Keeper, 1964, section of triptych. Margaret Seeler. Gold and silver cloisonné on copper, waxed matt finish; 6" × 4½" (section). In the collection of The Wichita Art Association, Inc.

Fig. 1-11 Susan. Lisel Salzer. Grisaille enamels on copper; 4" × 5¾".

National craft exhibits during the 1950s displayed fine examples of enamels by Karl Drerup, New Hampshire; Charles Bartley Jeffery, Ohio; Arthur and Jean Ames, California.

Relocating in the United States in the 1960s, Margaret Seeler, from the Academy of Fine Arts of Berlin, redefined the use of cloisonné.

Lisel Salzer of Washington studied historical grisaille enamels and now uses her interpretations in enamel portraits.

Oppi and Sara Untracht have contributed with their text and fine examples of enameling from all over the world.

John Paul Miller has studied the ancient technique of granulation on gold (see color section). Combining this technique with enamels, he produces naturalistic jewelry of exquisite beauty.

Using a less conventional approach, June Schwarcz of California has incorporated electroforming techniques and enameling to produce forms with tactile textures.

Unconventional firing techniques and mural-size enamels have been promoted by Paul Hultberg of Stony Point, New York.

William Harper of Florida excites the art collectors of New York with his exotic fetishes.

Impasto, camaïeu and grisaille have come alive in the hands of Harold B. Helwig of Kentucky.

On the West Coast of the U.S., large-scale environmental enamels have found their role in architecture. Fred Uhl Ball's panels and fascias involve the public on a daily basis.

Along with numerous other enamelists featured in these pages, all these artists bring their own sure quality and aesthetic approach to the current renaissance in enameling. The simple process of glass fired onto metal continues to fascinate, to inspire, to create exciting artifacts.

The characteristics of enamels

In simple terms, enamel is a special vitreous glass, colored with oxides. It is generally either opaque or transparent, and has properties specifically for application onto metal surfaces.

Fig. 1-12 *Bowl, 1980. June Schwarcz. Plique-à-jour Electroplated foil bowl, iron plated; 8" diameter, 5⅞" high.*

Fig. 1-13 Archangel Sebastian—The Mystic, 1982. William Harper. Pendant with chain; gold and silver cloisonné enamel on copper and fine silver; 24K and 14K gold, sterling silver, moonstone; 18.9 × 9.6 × 3.8 cm. Photograph, Kennedy Galleries, Inc.

Fig. 1-14 Sea Red, She Said. Harold B. Helwig. Limoges, transparent red and opaque white enamel with pure gold overlay details on cut copper; 24.8 cm. Photograph, the artist.

Fig. 1-15 The Way Home, 1981. Fred Uhl Ball. Titanium-based enamel fired on copper, which was premachined into 1,556 12-inch squares. Photograph, Bruce Beck. In the collection of the Sacramento Housing and Redevelopment Agency with the Sacramento Metropolitan Arts Commission.

Fig. 1-16 Glacial Rhythms, 1980. Pamela Harlow. Transparent enamels over opaque white on copper, gloss surface; 88" × 97½". Photograph, the artist.

Glass can be made by man, or found as a natural element of the earth. The most common form of natural glass is obsidian, which can be generated from a volcanic eruption. Upon solidification, the molten volcanic rock will cool to a glass (obsidian) or crystallize into rock, depending on its composition and cooling rate.

Glass has been classified as a liquid, as a solid, and as a gas. Glass scientists have differing theories and terminology to describe this matter. Glass can be changed from a liquid to a rigid state and will exhibit great plasticity at high temperatures while remaining rigid at low temperatures. Glass has no melting point. Under normal manufacturing conditions, glass will not crystallize and remains isotropic.

How enamels are made

Glass for enameling is manufactured specifically for application onto metals. A combination of raw materials is necessary to produce the brilliance of color, elasticity, coefficient of expansion and contraction, variances in firing temperatures and the other characteristics required to produce a quality product.

The clear glass (*flux, frit,* and *fondant* are other descriptive terms for this basic component) is basically silican dioxide, with additives of sodium, potassium, lithium, calcium, barium, lead, zinc, boron, titanium, and fluorine. These compounds are mixed in the formula proportions, placed in a crucible and heated to about 2200°F (1205°C) for a few hours. A viscous melt results. Some opaque enamels and lumps are made by sintering the raw materials together at lower temperatures for longer periods of time.

While in its molten state, the vitreous glass is poured into cold water or onto a steel block where, upon impact, the glass takes on its rigid state. It will then shatter into a lump form upon impact with the cold or wet. In the U.S., lump enamel is then ground with hardened steel rollers to the approximate 80-mesh size (0.0070 inch [177 microns]) of enamel that is marketed by enamel supply houses.

Classification

Three classifications designate the passage of light through enamels: opaque, opalescent, and transparent. These three types are now available in a choice of lead-bearing or lead-free enamels. In some instances,

Fig. 1-18 Column #2 with Coyote and Raven and Others, *Aperture Series. Colette. Transparent enamels on fine silver; 24K gold cloisonné wire, electroformed copper; 7" × 3½" × 3". Photograph, the artist.*

Fig. 1-17 Fallen Torso. *Jamie Bennett. Wall relief; opaque enamels, cloisonné and Limoges on steel and copper; 8" × 8" × 1". Photograph, the artist.*

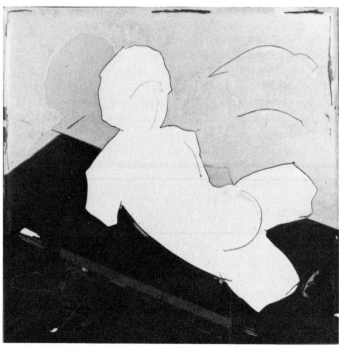

there is also a choice of firing temperatures: hard fusing, medium fusing and soft fusing.

OPAQUES

Opaque describes the characteristic of the fired enamel. After it is fired, the enamel is dense in opacifiers and does not permit the passage of light through the coating.

Opaque enamels are excellent for shading and, when used together with transparents, add depth and dimension to the latter's characteristics. An opaque enamel hides the host metal surface. Traditionally, opaques were used for champlevé.

When ground or sifted to 325 mesh or finer, opaque enamels are excellent painting enamels, especially for Limoges techniques.

TRANSPARENTS

The most seductive of all enamels, transparent and translucent enamels, allow the passage of light through to the host metal below. The combination of the transparency and the metallic surface intensifies the richness of the colors. Jewellike surfaces result from many thin applications of enamel. As the thickness of an enamel increases, its transparency decreases.

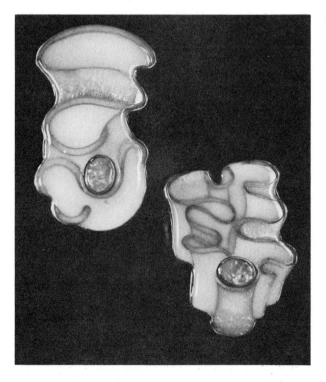

Fig. 1-19 *Pins. Connie Brauer. Opalescent enamels on fine silver and silver foils; opals set in sterling silver; $1\frac{3}{4}''$ × 1''. Photograph, the artist.*

Fig. 1-20 Crack of Bizarre Delights, 1982. David C. Freda. Enamels on copper, aluminum slate, sterling silver coccoon and hummingbird; 12" × 8" × 10".

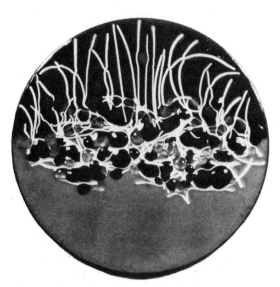

Fig. 1-21 Landscape Illusion. Pamela Carey Steele. Lump and thread enamels on copper; 9" diameter. Photograph, the artist.

OPALESCENTS

Opalescent aptly describes this third classification of enamels. The visual effect of the fired enamel is reminiscent of an opal. Opalescent enamel is basically a transparent enamel, with minor amounts of opacifiers added. The inclusion of opacifier causes less light to be absorbed into the surface and more light to be reflected, giving a tonal range to the colors.

Maturation temperatures

HARD-FUSING ENAMELS

Hard-fusing enamel (most often flux) is fired at 1500°F–1550°F (816°C–843°C).

MEDIUM-FUSING ENAMELS

Medium-fusing enamels are fired at 1450°F–1500°F (788°C–816°C). These are the most common of all the enamels.

SOFT-FUSING ENAMELS

A soft-fusing enamel has a firing temperature of 1400°F–1450°F (760°C–788°C).

Fig. 1-22 Parcels, 1980. Charlene Modena. Enameled copper, woven and electroformed; handmade paper, gold, iron mica; each parcel $1\frac{1}{2}'' \times 1\frac{1}{2}'' \times 6''$. Photograph, the artist.

LOW-FIRE ENAMELS

Low temperature enamel matures at 950°F–1050°F (510°C–566°C). Specifically manufactured for aluminum. Also can be used on sterling silver, stainless steel and brass.

Forms of enamel

LUMPS

Available in both transparent and opaque, lump enamel can be used for decorative and textural effects; alternatively, it can be ground with a mortar and pestle to the particle size required for the application at hand. Lump enamel has greater stability than finely ground enamels when stored for lengths of time. The deterioration of lump enamel is slower than that of the finer mesh sizes because the total surface exposure of each granule to the atmosphere is less.

THREADS

Available in opaque colors, enamel threads are just another formation of the glass. Although the threads often appear quite sculptural and three-dimensional, when heated to enameling temperatures, the forms will soften and conform to the surface onto which they have been placed.

ENAMELS IN MESH SIZES

Granular enamels are generally available in three mesh sizes:

1. 80 mesh (U.S. Standard)
2. 150 mesh (U.S. Standard) used in the badge-making industry
3. 325 mesh, painting grade (U.S. Standard)

Fig. 1-23 Amethyst Rainbow, 1981. Barbara Mail. 24K gold cloisonné on copper; 14K gold setting, amethyst, enameled, constructed; 1¾" × 1¾" × ½". Photograph, Rod McCormick.

Fig. 1-24 Daisy, 1979. Kathryn Regier Gough. Transparent and opaque enamels on gold foil; 14K gold setting, 8mm blue pearls; 3" × 3⅛". Photograph, the artist.

Mesh sizes describe the particle size of the enamel that will pass through U.S. Standard mesh sieve screens. For most applications 80 mesh (0.0070 inch [177 microns]) is used. Any enamel granule 80-mesh size to infinity that will pass through the designated screen is defined as 80 mesh.

Metals for enameling

The most common metals used in enameling are copper, fine silver, and high-karat golds. The thickness of these metals can vary considerably, according to the requirements of the individual artist. As a general rule 18 B & S Gauge (1.024 mm) metals are used; use of this gauge minimizes the warping that may occur as the enamel and the metal independently expand and contract during the firing and cooling processes.

Copper

Copper is an excellent metal to enamel upon. It is easy to use and gives relatively trouble-free results. Although bare copper oxidizes when heated, the scale can be removed with ease. Copper and 24-karat gold cloisonné wire are extremely compatible when used together for enameling.

Alloys of copper should be avoided; problems often arise when these alloys are fired many times, over extended periods.

Fine (pure) silver

Fine silver will not oxidize with successive firings and will remain bright. This characteristic is desirable when using transparents and opalescent colors. It is a most satisfying metal to use in combination with enamels and is worth the additional investment.

Sterling silver

Sterling silver is 925 parts fine silver to 75 parts copper; it is not recommended for general enameling purposes. After three or four firings during the enameling process, sterling will start to oxidize and leave a dark shadow underneath transparent or opalescent enamels. Fine silver, although a little more expensive, is worth every penny of its initial cost.

Sterling silver can be used when a fine silver surface is "brought up" to the metal surface; this is a time-consuming process for which instructions can be found in most jewelry or silversmithing books.

Some reds will change color when applied directly over silver, so transparent reds should be used with a flux underneath.

High-karat golds

The higher the karat of gold used, the more equisite the results. As it is uneconomical to recommend 24-karat gold to the average enamelist, consider using 24-karat gold foil over silver or copper.

As the base metal, 18 or 20 karat gold is quite acceptable, although gold cloisonné wire should be 24 karat for ease of bending.

Use only "green gold," which has no additives of copper or cadmium. These additives will oxidize and leave a dark shadow underneath the enamel surface.

Low grades of gold (14 karat and lower) also will oxidize with successive firings and are impractical unless the enamel is to be fired only once or twice.

Aluminum

Type 3003 or pure aluminum is most suitable for enameling. It can be purchased in small quantities through an enamel supplier, or in quantity at a local sheet metal warehouse.

Gilding metal

Gilding metal, an alloy of copper (95% cu and 5% zn), is used mainly by industry for badge making and signs. It looks and works basically like copper.

Iron and steel

Pre-enameled iron and steel tiles are available on today's market for the enamelist's use. These tiles can be purchased ready prepared, with white enamel over a dark ground coat, or with only a dark ground coat. Used extensively on building projects such as murals and wall panels, these tiles have the distinct advantage of minimum warpage.

When using steel or iron that has not been prepared by the supplier for enameling, as described above, the metal needs special preparation and a ground coat of enamel before enameling can proceed.

Fig. 1-25 The First Americans. *Jo Ann Tanzer. Limoges on steel; transparent and opaque enamels; 12″ × 12″. Photograph, the artist.*

Fig. 1-26 Brass Landscape, *1981. Fred Uhl Ball. Liquid enamels brushed over brass; 6″ × 8″. Photograph, Kurt Fishback.*

Stainless steel

Grades 304 and 410 stainless steel can be enameled with some lead-free and lead-bearing enamels. Stainless steel does not have to be ground-coated like enameling iron. Another advantage is that counter enameling is not necessary. Surfaces should be degreased, but do not need to be annealed before the enamel applications. Stamped shapes can be purchased from enamel suppliers.

Brass

Traditionally, brass is not used for enameling in the Western world. The chemical composition of the brass inhibits extended firing procedures. However, if willing to experiment, you can achieve exciting results; keep an open mind and approach this metal creatively.

Fig. 2-1 Handpiece with Elephant, One Bird and Two Geese, *Aperture Series. Colette. Brooch and neckpiece enclosed; cloisonné enamel, electroformed bronze, anodized aluminum; $4\frac{3}{4}''\times3\frac{3}{4}''\times5''$. Photograph, the artist. In the collection of Andrew Lewis.*

·2·
Materials, equipment and supplies

Starting a personal enameling record

A small sketchbook/notebook/scrapbook will become your most important tool. No prefessional artist would ever be without his sketchbook; it becomes almost an extension of one's self.

Into this compendium will go your ideas, sketches, pictures of things you like, designs and your innermost thoughts. Once you get into the habit of keeping a sketchbook, it is an excellent policy to have one for each year. Use hardbound (unruled) books that come from artist's supply stores; put the date on the spine; and keep each one close to your enameling bench.

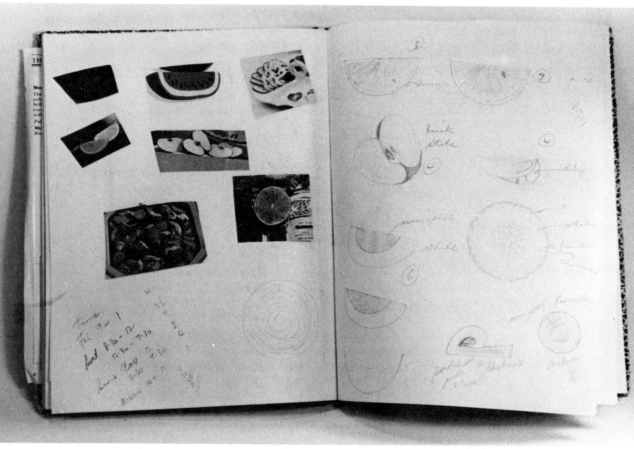

Fig. 2-2 *A working page from a sketchbook.*

Apart from your ideas and aspirations, compile an accurate log of each color and each step used for an enameling project. It all seems very clear now, but next year when you wish to achieve a similar effect, the memory cells will be short of instant recall. It also becomes an excellent reference source when an enamel needs repair work in years to come.

In the beginning, it may be difficult to think an enameling project through from start to finish—from a black-and-white sketch to a vibrant enamel. A good aid is to do an accurate drawing of the design, and use watercolor pencils or marking pens to color it as closely as possible to how you envision the finished color scheme. You will now be able to look at color harmonies, balance, and compatibility. This process will acquaint you with a different aspect of the design you have been thinking about. Do not forget to include the color of the metal, the surrounding edges, the cloisonné wires, mountings, and so on. The colors of these elements influence the colors you choose and the balance of the color application. When using transparent enamels, think of what will be reflected from the background metal and how it too will affect the proportions.

Do several sketches of the same design and alter color arrangements and schemes. Keep all these designs and notes in your book. Also record each firing: how long; what temperature; colors used; your responses; other people's reactions. All this is important information.

A good sketchbook can be your closest friend.

Supplies

The most fabulous studio in the world, with every piece of equipment ever made arranged in its correct place, will not necessarily produce

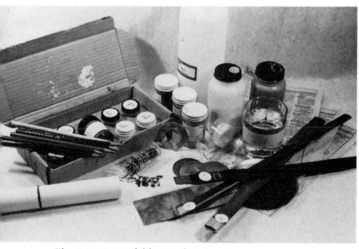

Fig. 2-3 *Expendable supplies for classroom use.*

Fig. 2-4 *Some of the preformed shapes available for enameling. Equipment courtesy of Seaire Manufacturing.*

great creative enamels. Of course, certain equipment is needed, but it is your creative drive and your wish to learn and grow that will produce the *pièce de résistance*.

Often, as a student starts in a classroom situation, all necessary large equipment is provided by the institution where the classes are held. Consequently, materials and equipment will be discussed in two categories: (1) basic needs while attending classes; and (2) materials needed to set up your own studio. These will include materials for enameling purposes only. If you are interested in combining jewelry making and silversmithing with your enameling, see the Further Reading list for a good reference on the necessities for a well-equipped metalworking studio.

For the classroom

Equipment and supplies needed while attending enameling classes
are based on the six step-by-step projects covered in Part Two.

EXPENDABLE SUPPLIES

Selection of 80-mesh enamels
Painting enamel kit
Underglaze pencils
Threads and lumps
Binder (Klyr-Fire or similar)
Scalex or similar
Distilled water
Tracing paper
Double-sided sticky tape
Carbon paper, 8008 Stabilo pencil
Emery paper: #1, #2/0, #4/0
Wet and dry paper: #320
Old telephone books or magazines
Metal:
    18 B & S gauge (1.024 mm) copper sheet
    cloisonné wire, fine silver, flat 18 × 30
      B & S gauge (1.024 mm × 0.255 mm)

TOOLS AND MATERIALS

Sketch book (see discussion on page 21)
Selection of good quality artist's brushes: #000
    to #12
One inexpensive #12 artist's brush
Needlenose tweezers, watchmaker's or
    jeweler's
Scribe
Nail scissors or solder scissors
Inlay tool set
Eye droppers (at least two)
Plastic spoons or small mixing containers
Three glass beakers for liquids
Linen cloths
Magnifying glasses
Atomizer, if desired

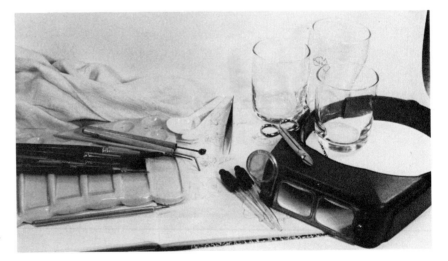

Fig. 2-5 *Supplies for classroom use.*

For your studio

EXPENDABLE SUPPLIES

Enamels:
    Selection of 80-mesh enamels
    Painting enamel kit
    Underglaze pencils

Fine line black
Underglaze D
Lusters
Oxides

Separation enamel
Threads and lumps
Liquid or crackle enamel
Binder (Klyr-Fire or similar)
Scalex or similar
Distilled water
Tracing paper
Double-sided tape
Carbon paper, Stabilo 8008 pencil
Emery paper: #1, #2/0, #4/0
Wet and Dry paper: #320
Old telephone books or magazines
Kiln wash
Pickle (Sparex, or nitric or sulphuric acid)
Powdered pumice
Pure liquid soap
Glass brush
Brass brush
Alundum stone
Heatless grinder (if you have a flex-shaft)
Diamond drill (if you have a flex-shaft)
Metal:
18 B & S gauge (1.024 mm) copper sheet
18 gauge (1.024 mm) fine silver sheet
cloisonné wire, fine silver 18 × 30; B & S gauge, (1.024 mm × 0.255 mm), flat
Silver and gold foils

BASIC EQUIPMENT AND TOOLS

Kiln with pyrometer
Kiln furniture
Kiln trowel
Heat-resistant surface (ceramic kiln shelf is excellent)

Pickle pot
Nonferrous metal tongs
Good exhaust system
Good light source
Sifters:
80 mesh, various sizes
80–325 mesh grading set
Heat-resistant gloves
Special safety glasses
Press plate (optional)
Magnifying glasses
Porcelain or agate mortar and pestle: large porcelain for grinding; small agate for painting
Glass beakers for liquids; at least three
Dental tools
Linen cloths
Scribe
Plastic spoons or mixing containers
Atomizer, if desired
Jeweler's hand tools:
Rawhide or wood mallet
Hand drill or flex-shaft
Files #2 and #4
Pliers: Round-nose and flat-nose watchmaker's or jeweler's pliers, both with highly polished jaws
Nail scissors or solder snips
Needlenose watchmaker's or jeweler's tweezers
Hand vise
Jeweler's saw or metal shears
Jeweler's saw blades, #2/0
Bench pin

Kilns

Buying a kiln is a major investment; its size and specifications will depend entirely on your well-thought-out needs. It would be uneconomical to buy a large kiln with a firing chamber 18 × 18 × 9 inches (456 × 456 × 228 mm) when you are primarily interested in producing small enamels no larger than 2 inches × 2 inches (51 mm × 51 mm) for jewelry.

Before purchasing this major piece of equipment, research all the possibilities. Talk to people: ask enamelists you know and don't know about *their* kilns; inquire at the local university or arts guild; talk to kiln suppliers.

Requirements

A few basic features must be included in whatever kiln you decide upon:

1. A pyrometer for quick temperature reference.

2. A temperature-control gauge that you can manipulate to maintain constant temperatures.

3. A front-opening door that swings from east to west (unless you are left-handed, in which case you want the reverse). This type of door is much easier to handle than a north–south opening kiln.

4. When determining the size kiln you need, the enamel and trivet assemblage should not be closer to any side than 1 inch (24 mm).

Overextend yourself. Buy a kiln that is a little more expensive than you really would like to pay, and a little bigger than you really need. As you grow as an enamelist, your needs will be more demanding; a kiln bought today will be less expensive than one bought five years from now.

Forget about hobby kilns. You will outgrow one of these before you finish the six basic projects in Part Two. Be conscious of utility efficiency; different kilns run on different voltages and this must be taken into consideration when setting up a home studio. Whatever kiln you decide upon, treat it with respect. The kiln is the key to your enameling success. A messy kiln will more than likely produce messy enamels. Pride in your equipment shows, just like pride in your work.

When you first obtain your kiln, work with it, even when it is not turned on. Become acquainted with it like you would a new friend; talk to it, love it. The kiln will respond and produce wonderful results if you believe in it. A good kiln is a great investment.

Cleaning and maintenance

Never use your kiln for anything other than enameling. Do not use it as a burn-out kiln for silversmithing; do not heat your lunch in it; an enameling kiln is used only for enameling.

The kiln should be kept as clean as possible. The traditional method is to "wash" the kiln with kiln wash. Usually the floor is the only part of the kiln needing this treatment. Kiln wash (50% flint: 50% kaolin) can be bought from any ceramic supply house. It is a powder that you mix with water to a thick, creamy consistency. Paint the floor of the _cold_ kiln with an even coat and allow to dry about 30 minutes before heating the kiln. This coating protects the expensive kiln floor from enamel spillage. Any enamel that is spilt adheres to the kiln wash, not the kiln floor. When the kiln is cool, the kiln wash with the adhered enamel can be scraped away, leaving the floor clean and undamaged. Without this protection, enamel sticks fast to the kiln floor and either

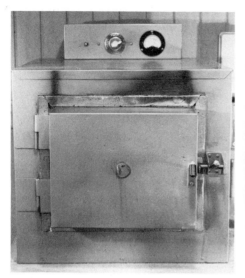

Fig. 2-7 *Kiln with north-south opening door.*

Fig. 2-6 *Kiln with a pyrometer and east-west opening door.*

has to be chipped away, perhaps damaging the surface, or left as a sticky mess during future firings. The little time it takes to carry out this simple maintenance pays off over and over again.

A new product on the market is a thin blanket of fire-retardent material for kiln floors. This material is bought from your enameling supplier and can be fitted into the bottom of the firing chamber. It is relatively inexpensive and, when the blanket becomes contaminated, it can be thrown away and a new blanket put in the kiln.

Kiln furniture

Kiln furniture is essential to the success of your enameling. You must always use the right trivet for the job; it is difficult to compromise and still obtain excellent results. You will never regret investing in a comprehensive collection of trivets and stilts. If you don't have the right one available, make one from stainless steel. It is better to take the time to do this correctly than to spend hours repairing trivet marks on your enamels.

Trivets often become contaminated with the excess enamels that may fall onto their surfaces during use. Before each firing, a trivet should be cleaned of any enamel drips by stoning or hammering. If you choose to hammer the excess enamel off a trivet, be careful to protect your eyes from the flying glass particles. (Trivets and their uses are discussed in more detail in chapter 4.)

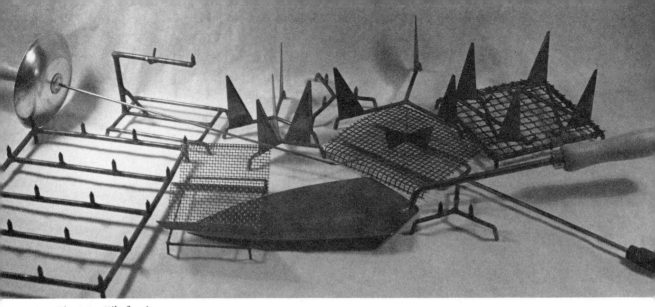

Fig. 2-8 *Kiln furniture: trivets, planches, trowels. Some equipment courtesy of Seaire Manufacturing.*

Safety equipment and procedures

Almost anything can be a health hazard. Safety procedures are not discussed here to alarm you or to deter you from enameling, but to make you aware of the precautions that should be taken. The best safety rule is prevention. If something does happen, Do Not Panic, take three deep breaths, think, and then panic! Seriously, most safety precautions are just good common sense; by being aware of the measures you can take to protect yourself, many happy hours can be spent enameling without any risk to your health.

In recent years, several publications have been written on the subject of health in the arts; the Center for Occupational Hazards produces a newsletter if you want an in-depth current source of safety information: Art Hazards Newsletter, published by the Center for Occupational Hazards, Inc., 5 Beekman St., New York, N.Y., 10088 ($10/year).

Enamel application

Many of the enamels on the market today are lead-bearing. Used on a small scale with reasonable precautions, it is not incorrect to say that these enamels pose little risk to the user. However, when occasional use turns into production, all factors are multiplied.

Within the past few years there has been an increase in the variety of lead-free enamels available. They are of comparable quality to lead-bearing enamels, and the choice now lies entirely with the user.

When sifting or applying any enamel, it is advisable to follow a few simple rules, not only as a courtesy to fellow workers, but also for your own health. When sifting enamels, always use a clean sheet of paper for catching excess. Slowly and carefully pour the excess back into the container so a cloud of dust is not created. Fold the paper (do not wad it) and discard. Old magazines or newspapers or telephone book pages make excellent catchalls. After one use they can be discarded without any feeling of extravagance.

Anything that goes into your mouth—food, drink, cigarettes, etc.—can be a depository for the fine dust that pollutes the air while sifting enamels. Keep your bodily needs separated from your artistic endeavors. It does not hurt to relax every once in a while for a cup of coffee—away from the studio area.

Good ventilation in the studio is always a premium. Good ventilation is a must near the kiln, and in pickling and soldering areas. It is certainly not advisable to work in a small closet or darkroom-type space or basement area where there is no fresh air. If you have any respiratory disease or difficulties, wear a dust mask or respirator whenever you work with enamels.

Working with acids

There are several basic rules to always follow when using chemicals. Although any chemical—and especially acids—must be handled with great respect, there is no reason to avoid their use, as long as you are aware of potential danger.

WARNING: There are three all-important considerations when working with acids:

1. *Acids should never be mixed together* under any circumstances. The resulting gases may be lethal.
2. Most undiluted acids used for enameling and silversmithing will immediately burn holes in skin, clothing, and equipment. While diluted acids still have the same potential, it will take considerably longer.
3. Fumes from undiluted acids can burn your respiratory passages.

Acid containers should be labeled correctly and stored in a safe place. Keep out of reach of children and animals. It is a good policy to store them on the bottom shelf, or at ground level. This way they cannot be knocked from the shelf and broken.

Most of the acids enamelists use can be neutralized with sodium bicarbonate (baking soda). Keep several boxes on hand—one at each work station. In an emergency, if baking soda is not available, club soda can be used as a weak substitute.

When using acids, always maintain good ventilation. So often craftsmen work in confined spaces, usually converted from other uses. If there is no facility for an exhaust fan, be certain to use a conventional fan in conjunction with an open window to disperse concentrated fumes.

Disposal of waste acids should be handled carefully. Small amounts of pickling solution can be neutralized with sodium bicarbonate, diluted with large quantities of water and flushed or poured away. Never put pickle straight down a drain. The acid will attack all nonferrous metal pipes and corrode them. *Never pour flammable liquids down a drain! The resulting fumes can produce a pipe bomb.*

Some etchants are never disposable and will always be a hazardous waste, whether they remain in a container or are poured down a drain or onto the ground. It is advisable to contact your local state health organization for regulations and advice before you purchase acids.

Heating equipment

Because enamelists use extreme heat for firing enamels and annealing metal, it is advisable to have a fire extinguisher on hand. If you are working in a classroom situation, know where the fire extinguisher is kept and whether in your studio or a classroom, *know how the fire extinguisher works.*

Wherever you work, it is not advisable to use asbestos. Asbestos is known to be a carcinogen and a dangerous health hazard. Fortunately, there are many alternatives available.

ANNEALING PANS

An ideal annealing arrangement is a commercially available annealing pan full of pumice rock (a fire retardant) with several large charcoal blocks to support the metal (Fig. 2-9). If this arrangement is too expensive or too large, an inexpensive alternative is to use an aluminum

Fig. 2-9 *A commercial annealing pan with pumice rock and charcoal blocks.*

Fig. 2-10 *Low-cost annealing pan with pumice rock and charcoal block.*

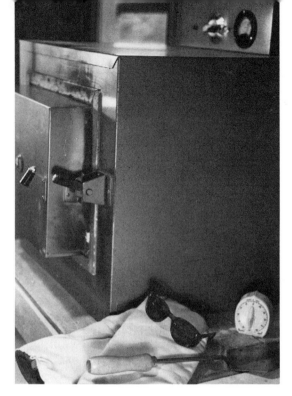

Fig. 2-11 *Heat-resistant kiln mittens, special safety glasses; note the use of a long-handled kiln trowel, and a ceramic kiln shelf as heat-resistant surface.*

pie pan, again filled with pumice rock and charcoal blocks as supports. Commercial annealing pans usually rotate—a decided advantage. The same effect can be achieved by placing your pie pan on a lazy susan (Fig. 2-10); this will rotate quite satisfactorily. Providing that your pieces are not huge, this alternative should serve you well for many years.

HEAT-RESISTANT SURFACES

For complete silversmithing and annealing safety precautions, read any good silversmithing book (see Further Reading list).

When taking pieces out of the kiln, it is necessary to place the trivet assemblage onto a heat-resistant surface. An ideal flat surface to use is a commercially available kiln shelf, the type used in larger ceramic kilns. Have two: one on which to place hot trivets, and the other to use for flattening the hot, warped enamels. A bare concrete floor will serve well for the latter use, but floors are often treated with some type of coating that could be flammable. A flat steel plate is another alternative. A separate area for flattening the warped pieces is recommended. It keeps the hot enamels away from the kiln, which may be in use by others.

Firebricks (the kind used for ceramic kiln building) make an excellent stand for the kiln so it is not in direct contact with any normal countertop surface. A ceramic kiln shelf would also serve this purpose well.

GLOVES

When using a kiln, remember that the temperatures inside are at least four times greater than any food cooking temperature normally used. You would never take a pot or pan out of your oven without adequate protection. Similarly, you must protect yourself when manipulating enamels and equipment to and from the kiln. It is wise to wear long-sleeved flame-retardant clothing. Natural fibers are the first choice. If this seems impractical, keep a long-sleeved pure cotton smock in your studio to be worn while enameling (it will also help protect your everyday wear). *Wear long-sleeved flame-resistant gloves on both hands.* If an emergency arises, you may need two hands. There is no longer any need to buy asbestos gloves, as there are excellent alternatives available. Often these mittens or gloves are too large for a woman's hand. Try wearing them on the opposite hand, e.g., left on right and vice-versa. This will give better contact between the glove and the hand.

SAFETY GLASSES

Recently, medical researchers have warned that infrared light may cause cataracts. Every time you look into a kiln, there is a concentration of heat-containing infrared rays hitting your eyes. Special safety glasses in dark and extra dark can be worn as protection against this potential hazard.

Fig. 3-1 45th Parallel: Halfway between the North Pole and the Equator, *1981. Cheri Epstein. Wallpiece, cloisonné enamel, fine silver, silk, Plexiglas, copper; 8″ × 6½″ × ¼″. Photograph, the artist.*

·3·
Preparation of enamels and metals

Traditionally, enamel was bought in lumps and only the quantity to be used immediately was ground to the required particle size. The larger the particles, the slower the deterioration of the enamel. As the lumps were ground with a mortar and pestle, often underwater, the enamel was automatically washed during the grinding process.

Today, most enamelists purchase their enamels preground to 80-mesh particle size. In the U.S., the lump is ground with hardened steel rollers. This crushing process does not produce uniform particles. Consequently, when a bottle of 80-mesh enamel is purchased, the bottle will also contain enamel of much finer mesh sizes. When you look into a bottle of enamel, there appears to be finer, whiter-looking powder on top. This is the finely ground enamel which enamelists often wash away, but it can be used for painting. It can be reclaimed from the 80-mesh enamel—along with other size particles—by sifting, leaving the largest granules for that special transparent application. This sifting process is an excellent alternative to washing enamels. Specific information may be found in *Glass on Metal* (vol. 1, no. 2; March, 1982).

"The larger the particle size, the greater the transparency," has long been an enameling rule. This is basically true, but the increased particle size of the enamel introduces two variables into the firing process. There must be a temperature/time increase to mature the larger granules, plus the surface coverage may not be as complete. These factors increase the possibility of the metal surface oxidizing before the applied enamel matures. This can be observed as red-copper oxide outlines, and can be alleviated if a regular 80-mesh base coat of flux is applied first. A thin coat of ungraded enamel will also achieve the desired results.

Opaques are very rarely washed or sifted, unless they are contaminated with foreign matter. The different particle sizes actually aid in the firing process, so in most cases it is to the enamelist's advantage not to sift or wash opaques.

Screen separation of enamels

Screen separation of enamel is achieved by the following technique. Place five sifters, one inside the other: on the bottom use a collecting pan, followed by a 325-mesh sifter; a 200-mesh sifter; a 100-mesh sifter; an 80-mesh sifter and a 60-mesh sifter on top (Fig. 3-2). Place a lump or two of enamel in each sifter to help speed up the process of sifting

Fig. 3-2 *U.S. Standard Mesh sifting pans: 60 mesh, 80 mesh, 100 mesh, 200 mesh, 325 mesh, catch pan on bottom.*

and to keep the screens from becoming blocked. Empty a quantity of 80-mesh enamel of your selected color into the top sifter. Gently tap the sides of the stacked sifters; the enamel will fall through the screens according to particle size. This may take several minutes to complete.

Eventually you will have five or six grades of enamel: greater than 60 mesh; 80 mesh; 100 mesh; 200 mesh; and 325 mesh, which will be gathered in the collecting pan. This 325-mesh enamel is ideal for painting techniques.

The 80-mesh or larger mesh enamels are now free of all the "fines" and are in excellent condition; they should require no washing and the transparent enamels are especially transparent. The finer mesh enamels are ready for use for other applications. Bottle and label these enamels according to their particle size.

Washing enamels

Wash only what you need today. Opaques should not require washing; opalescents and transparents can be washed for greater transparency.

Put a small quantity of the enamel in a clear glass beaker and add about three to four times that amount of water. Stir thoroughly with a glass rod. The enamel acts as an abrasive and, if you use metal or plastic as a stirrer, small particles of metal or plastic can contaminate the enamel. The mixture will become cloudy. This is caused by the smallest particles (fines) of the enamel. Let the large particles settle for a moment, then drain off the cloudy water. Repeat this operation several times, until the water is clear and the remaining larger grains of enamel sparkle. There will be some enamel lost, but that is the price you pay for washing. For the final washing, use distilled water. Tap water usually contains minerals and other deposits.

Empty the washed enamel into a small container. Mark the container with the enamel color and number. The wet enamel can be used immediately in its wet state or allowed to dry. While drying, cover the container with a piece of cloth so that dust in the atmosphere will not fall into the freshly washed enamels.

An alternate method is to substitute alcohol for water during the washing process. It evaporates readily, minimizing the length of time an enamel is exposed to moisture. Recent studies have shown that prolonged exposure to water will deteriorate a ground enamel much quicker than normal atmospheric conditions. Use ethyl or grain (ethanol) alcohol (methyl or wood alcohols are poisonous if taken internally, or breathed as fumes).

Cleaning and pickling metal

There are two basic methods of preparing metal for enameling: (1) acid bath or pickling (Fig. 3-6); and (2) burn-off or annealing (Fig. 3-7).

Fig. 3-3 *Wash enamel in distilled water, using a glass stirring rod as an agitator.*

Fig. 3-4 *Wash enamel until it sinks to the bottom and the water in the container is clear.*

Fig. 3-5 *Empty the washed enamel into a small container.*

As a general rule, use the acid bath method on small pieces of metal and the burn-off method for larger forms.

Most often, copper will be covered with a grease or oil coating (sometimes not visible) when purchased from the supplier. Pickling does not remove oily substances, but the subsequent scrubbing with pumice will. The pickling solution will remove metal and metal oxides (firescale). Small copper forms are usually not badly contaminated with grease, so eliminating the annealing process will help speed the initial preparation.

After larger pieces have been annealed, they too must be pickled to remove the metal oxides (firescale) that have formed during the annealing process.

Preparing an acid bath

Various acids can be used for the pickle. Nitric, hydrochloric, or sulfuric acids will all remove black copper oxides and red copper oxides. The commercial crystalline acid salt, Sparex, is a relatively safe acid to use. (If children are working with enameling materials, a combination of common household salt and vinegar is recommended.)

WARNING: *All acids must be treated with utmost caution.* If the acid splashes on your skin or clothing, the area should be flushed immediately with water, followed by a dusting of sodium bicarbonate (household baking soda), which will neutralize the acid. The diluted acid should not be strong enough to burn your skin, but it can still make holes in clothing and damage other surfaces.

Fig. 3-6 *Acid bath or pickle used for copper cleaning.*

Fig. 3-7 *Burn-off or annealing to remove oil and grease from copper.*

Nitric, hydrochloric and sulfuric acids are normally bought in a liquid form. They all need to be diluted with water before being used as a pickling solution. Never mix two acids together: *the resulting fumes can be lethal.*

A solution of one part acid to nine parts water makes an excellent pickling solution. <u>*Water must not be added to the concentrated acid.*</u> Pour water into a Pyrex container, ceramic slowcooker or commercial pickle pot. Slowly add the correct amount of acid, stirring occasionally. Trickle the acid down the inside rim of the bowl so it does not splash or boil.

Use only nonferrrous metal or wood tongs in the acid. Ferrous metals will create a galvanizing reaction, giving any metal placed in the bath a copper coating.

Sparex, a commercial acid salt, is an easier and safer acid to use. Following the manufacturer's instructions, mix the crystals into hot water and dissolve in a nonmetallic container. The solution reacts faster when used warm. Either a crock or pickle pot will keep the pickle warm without boiling. *When any type of pickle boils, it gives off toxic fumes.* Use only nonferrous metal or wooden tongs in Sparex for manipulating the metal projects to and from the bath.

All work with acids should be carried out in a well-ventilated area: this means moving air, not just an open window. Acid fumes are most harmful to the lungs. Always mark an acid container with its contents. If you have sensitive skin, wear rubber gloves. Keep the acid covered when it is not being used. Always keep baking soda (sodium bicarbonate) on hand in case of an emergency. It should be added to the acid solution, which will eventually become ineffective, before disposal.

Pickling step by step

1. To clean copper (or other selected metal), place it in the prepared pickle for approximately 5 minutes, or until it is a clean bright color. Remove the disc from the bath with nonferrous metal or wooden tongs and wash off the pickle under running water.

2. Using your fingers as an applicator, apply powdered pumice to the surface of the metal. Scrub vigorously, working methodically over the surfaces. If you have trouble achieving a bright, clean surface, scrub the metal with a fiberglass brush, again working under running water. A final wipe with saliva helps to alkalize the surface. Baking soda can be used as an alternative neutralizer.

3. When the metal looks completely clean, it is possible to make a quick test for confirmation. Slowly run clear water onto the surface of the disc; if the water "draws up" and lies in puddles or beads, the surface of the metal still carries oily residue; if the water lies in a complete sheet over the surface, the metal is clean and ready for enameling.

Annealing

The most effective way to rid copper of oil and grease contaminants is by burning the residues from the surface. Most enameling texts suggest that this process be done in the kiln, but if you wish to keep your kiln in excellent enameling condition, it is *not* advisable. Any dirt particles, soot or firescale that may come off the copper will remain in the kiln as small contaminants. Later, while firing a beautiful, trouble-free enamel, these floating particles can be deposited on the maturing enamel surface. They will appear as black specks from kiln furniture, green spots from copper oxides, and so on, thus destroying all your careful work. If you do use your kiln for annealing, remember that when you anneal copper to "green," copper oxide firescale will not form. Firescale on copper only "pops off" the surface during the cooling stages, or when the metal is returned to the kiln after the cooling process has commenced.

A wax burn-out kiln can be used as an annealing kiln; however, annealing copper with either an acetylene, natural-gas-and-air, or propane torch is the easiest of methods. It also has the advantage of enabling you to observe all that is taking place. It is not necessary to heat a copper form to red-hot temperatures. The higher the heat, the greater the copper oxide and firescale deposit. Heating to a dull charcoal grey or "green" is sufficient, as the purpose is to burn off oily contaminants, not to soften the metal.

When this has been achieved, let the copper form cool, brush off any loose firescale, and place the form into the pickle bath. (It is not advisable to put the very hot copper into the pickle; the pickle will react with the hot metal and may splash on you.) Pickle the copper

Fig. 3-8 *Scrub the surface with powdered pumice.*

Fig. 3-9 *Scrub metal with a fiberglass brush for a bright, clean surface.*

Fig. 3-10 *When the water draws up and lies in a puddle as shown, the metal surface is still not clean and free of residue.*

until the surface is a bright pink color. Proceed with the pumice and water treatment described in step 2 under Pickling.

Preparation of silver and gold

Fine silver and 24-karat gold do not normally require pickling unless they have become contaminated in some way. Fine silver, sterling silver, and gold are easily cleaned in the acid pickle process as described for copper if that is necessary. If you are using copper in your studio as well as silver and gold, it is advisable to have two separate pickle containers; one for the copper and one for the precious metals (silver and gold).

Finish the silver and gold surfaces with a fiberglass brush for extra brightness. A highly reflective surface looks excellent under transparents.

Silver and gold can be annealed to rid the surface of contaminants in the same manner described for copper. If cloisonné wire is to be annealed to restore flexibility, bind short coils together with binding wire (Fig. 3-11). This helps distribute heat evenly. Remove the binding wire before placing the annealed wire into the pickle.

Cleaning aluminum

For enameling surfaces, use only pure aluminum or #3003 alloy. Aluminum does not need to be pickled or annealed. Vitrearc Aluminum Cleaner, a powder that mixes with water, is scoured over the surface with a clean rag. This is the only cleaning necessary. Do not use household cleaners that contain chlorine. When the aluminum surface is bright, flush well with water and dry with a lint-free cloth.

Fig. 3-11 *Annealing fine silver cloisonné wire to restore its flexibility.*

Fig. 3-12 *Jewelers' emery papers and files for refining metal surfaces.*

Refining metal surfaces

When transparent enamels are to be used, it is necessary to take a close look at the metal surface before application. Any surface imperfections, such as scratches, will show through the transparent enamels. These imperfections need to be removed, preferably before pickling, although quite often scratches are not apparent until after the metal has been pickled, cleaned, and fiberglass-brushed.

Most scratches can be eliminated by careful papering with emery paper or wet and dry papers. Use several grades to refine the surface. When scratches are deeper, use a #2 file, followed by a #4 file until the surface is devoid of imperfections. Use a flat hand file on flat surfaces; round files for curved surfaces. Avoid any file that will alter the contour of the metal surface. Refine the filing marks with the various grades of emery cloth, as above.

Bright Boy rubber abrasive wheels on a flex-shaft or buffing motor can be used for a final semi-matt surface. Lea compound, a greaseless buffing compound applied to an electric buffing wheel, will produce an excellent shine. A final scouring of the surface with a fiberglass brush used under running water will also produce an excellent metal finish.

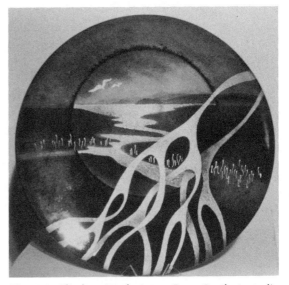

Fig. 4-1 Flinders Bowl. *Jenny Gore, South Australia. Transparent and opaque enamels, fine silver wires, silver foils; 16½" diameter. Photograph, the artist.*

· 4 ·
Firing procedures

Firing is one of the most important and critical steps in the process of making an enamel. Generally, the prepared project is fired in an electric enameling kiln kept especially for this purpose (see Chapter 1). On occasion, a silversmithing torch may be used. Whatever the source, heat is needed to transform the enamel particles into a continuous coating of vitreous glass over the host metal.

Using trivets, stilts and planches

One of the most important steps is selecting the correct trivet for the best results. A trivet too large, too small, or the wrong shape can damage a carefully prepared project.

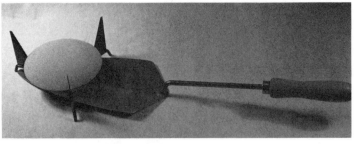

Fig. 4-3 *Fire the underside of a bowl on a winged trivet. Trivet and trowel, courtesy of Seaire Manufacturing.*

Fig. 4-2 *Trivet wings should only touch the bare edges of an enamel. Trivet, courtesy of Seaire Manufacturing.*

Fig. 4-4 *Place bowl on a star trivet or bowl stilt when firing the inside surface of a bowl. Trivet and trowel, courtesy of Seaire Manufacturing.*

A trivet is usually made from stainless steel. There are many useful shapes available commercially, but when you don't have one suitable for the job, you can improvise and make one to suit the purpose.

The trivet wings should touch only the bare edges of the enameling project (Fig. 4-2). If the wings touch the enamel, they will fire into the surface and you will have to break them away when the project cools. This will leave long, ugly scars to be repaired before any further firings take place.

For a curved shape, such as a bowl, fire the underside on a winged trivet. When firing the inside, place the bowl on a star trivet or bowl stilt. A four-prong stilt gives greater stability than a three-prong stilt.

With flat shapes, the size of the enamel project is an important factor. Small flat shapes can be fired on winged trivets without much trouble, but larger shapes need extra support to keep the flat sheet from *excessive* warping when heated. Seaire firing planches for firing flat panels are exceptionally good to use. Although there will be a series of small marks on the counter enamel, these planches give extra support to the enameling project. The planche also allows the metal to expand without resistance. If both sides of the enamel will be on view, an alternative is recommended.

Very small shapes, samples, and so on, can be fired on grooved trivets. This way, more than one enameled piece can be fired at once. There is a problem with this method of firing: the more pieces fired at once, the more problems you can have at once.

You must be able to place a kiln trowel or fork underneath whatever trivet you select so it can be lifted to and from the kiln. A legless trivet should be placed on a wire mesh planche that has a suitable space for the lifting equipment. Or, long tongs can be used but they tend to be awkward; manipulating tongs while your hands are covered in long fire-resistant gloves is quite clumsy.

Firing an enamel

When preparation of the enamel project is complete and the applied enamel is dry, the most critical steps have arrived. Preheat the kiln; it is advisable to have the temperature 50°F–100°F (10°C–20°C) higher than needed. When the kiln door is opened, there will be some heat loss, bringing the temperature down to the correct firing degree. Always have the kiln turned up during the firing procedure.

Place the project on the trivet most suitable for the piece. Add a mesh planche if the stainless steel trivet does not have a recessed area for the trowel or kiln fork to slip under. The assemblage is now ready to be placed into the kiln.

With the trowel or kiln fork, gently lift the enamel/trivet assemblage and place it in the center, toward the back of the preheated kiln. Do this as quickly as possible. The less time the door is open, the less heat is lost. While executing this operation, protect yourself against the heat by wearing long-sleeved flame-resistant clothing, long heat-resistant gloves and correct safety glasses to protect your eyes. Fire the enamel for approximately $1\frac{1}{2}$ to 2 minutes; remove the assemblage

Fig. 4-6 Small enamels can be fired in groups on a grooved trivet. Trivet courtesy of Seaire Manufacturing.

Fig. 4-5 Large, flat enamels need extra support—use a flat planche. Planche and trowel, courtesy of Seaire Manufacturing.

Fig. 4-7 A trivet without space for a kiln trowel or fork must be placed on a mesh rack or planche.

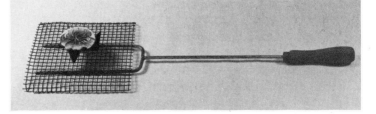

Fig. 4-9 "Orange peel" surface on a slightly underfired enamel.

Fig. 4-8 Placing an enamel project in the kiln, using correct kiln furniture. Trivet and trowel, courtesy of Seaire Manufacturing.

from the kiln using the same method. Place the trivet assemblage on a heat-resistant surface.

The length of time required for firing may vary according to weather conditions, size of the kiln, size of the project, and job at hand; therefore, it is good practice to check the firing process after about 1½ minutes. Do not open the kiln door wide: this will let out too much heat and, if the enamel has not matured, extra time will be required to build up the correct temperature again. The tiny opening in the kiln door should *not* be used as an observation hole. Looking into the kiln through this hole could damage your eyesight, especially if you are wearing contact lenses.

The following stages can be observed as an enamel surface reaches maturity: after about 1½ minutes at 1400°F–1500°F (760°C–816°C), the enamel will turn black and its granular quality will be most apparent; a short time later it will begin to glow slightly and take on an orange-peel appearance, resembling the skin of an orange (Fig. 4-9); finally, a few seconds later, the piece will take on a soft red glow from its inner heat and the enamel will have a shiny, liquid like quality. At this point, the enamel has fired to maturity and is ready for removal from the kiln.

Remove the enamel/trivet assemblage from the kiln with the kiln trowel or fork. Protect yourself again with the correct gloves and glasses. Check the surface of the enamel immediately after removal; if it has the orange-peel effect, it can be returned immediately to the kiln and firing continued for another 30 seconds or so. If the orange-peel surface is not too craterous, however, it can be ignored and will correct itself when the next coat is fired.

If you observe that the enamel surface has pulled away from the edges of the metal, the pieces may have been overfired, causing the enamel to burn away, leaving bare copper exposed. Another cause of the enamel pulling away from the edge can be attributed to heavy or irregular application of the enamel. See Chapter 12 for rectification. When pinholes and pits are evident, again refer to the troubleshooting section in Chapter 12.

The first few minutes after an enamel is removed from the kiln are always exciting. Colors often seem completely different from what you remembered. As the enamel cools, you will observe slow and subtle change to its true color and beauty.

Place the hot enamel assemblage away from other unfired work on a heat-resistant surface in an area devoid of drafts. This is a courtesy to fellow workers (if any), as well as protection for your own work. As the enamel cools, small black flakes of metal oxides (firescale) can pop off the bare copper edges, float through the air and land on other unfired pieces in the vicinity. This contaminant will cause unsightly spots and pits when the enamel is refired. A hot enamel which cools too rapidly because of sudden temperature changes will sometimes crack and craze from these extremes.

It is a good idea for the inexperienced enamelist to practice picking up the enamel/trivet assemblage with the kiln trowel or fork, carrying the unit and placing it down gently. Placing the assemblage into the kiln tends to take more time than expected and, while the kiln door is open, the temperature drops. The goal is to keep the kiln door open for the least time possible, thus maintaining an even inside temperature.

A kitchen (minute) timer is a useful piece of equipment in the enameling studio. When the enamel goes into the kiln, the timer can be set and the audible reminder is often welcomed. So often an enamel is overfired because of neglectful timing. *Do not leave the kiln area.* Stand with the kiln trowel in your hand to remind you of your committment, and resist the urge to talk. Remember that your enamel if firing.

Another casualty of firing comes from the project falling off the trivet onto the floor of the kiln. Panic will not help. Calmly pick up a pair of pliers or tongs, reach into the kiln with your hand protected by a long, fire-resistant glove and remove the project from the kiln. Then, go back and remove the trivet. Under no circumstances let the enamel project touch the electric wiring of the kiln: the impact can damage both the kiln and the artwork. Any unfired enamel that falls onto the kiln floor will still mature and become a sticky mess. This mess must be cleaned up and the floor treated with kiln wash.

Temperature control

There are many variables and few rules to firing an enamel project. Length of time and relative temperature are dependent on each other, and both can vary for the following reasons:

1. Size of the kiln interior in relation to the size of the piece.
2. Thickness of the metal; its shape, size, and type; whether copper, silver, or gold.
3. Thickness of the enamel coating and its type: soft-fusing, medium or hard-fusing.
4. Prevailing weather conditions and the insulation properties of the kiln.
5. The position of the enamel in the kiln during firing; e.g., close to the door is the coolest part.
6. Type of trivet arrangement used; some trivets absorb a great amount of heat.

High (hard) firing

The hotter the temperature, the greater the clarity of transparents. Higher temperatures also help to eliminate trapped bubbles in the enamel surface. The disadvantages of high (hard) firings are:

1. The base metal may not be able to withstand the higher temperature or cloisonné wires may melt. Remember, fine silver melts at 1761°F (960°C).
2. The enamel may pull away from the edges of the metal with the rapid softening of the surface.
3. There may be an unwanted change in colors. Opaque reds and some opaque yellows are particularly bad; they tend to burn out and appear black when fired too high, too often, or too long.
4. Rapid expansion of the metal may cause greater warping than would normally be experienced.

Low firing

Firing temperatures that are too low may cause the following problems:

1. The base metal may oxidize before the enamel matures. This can show up as a color change or by lack of adhesion between enamel and metal.
2. Cracking or crawling between coats, as the coats of enamel may not bond.
3. Insufficient heat may deter cracks or repairs from healing correctly, leaving the repairs still visible.

Fig. *4-10* Cityscape triptych. *Shirley Rosenthal. High-fired opaques on copper sections; mounted on Plexiglas; 72" × 24". Photograph, the artist.*

Some useful guidelines

Considering that each project has its own set of variables, the correct firing formula will come only with experience. As a rule of thumb, general firing temperatures are:

Soft-fusing enamels: 1400°F–1450°F (760°C–788°C)

Medium-fusing enamels: 1450°F–1500°F (788°C–816°C)

Hard-fusing enamels: 1500°F–1600°F (816°C–871°C)

Most enameling kilns are equipped with a pyrometer (temperature gauge). The pyrometer is connected to a thermocouple which records the inside temperature of the kiln, but a pyrometer gauge should be considered an approximation only. With a little practice, you will develop the skill of judging the correct firing temperature with your eyes.

Fig. *4-11* *Bowl, 1979. June Schwarcz. Enamels and electroplating; 3" high, 6" diameter. Photograph, the artist.*

Fig. 4-12 *Brooch. Belle and Roger Kuhn.*
Transparent enamels on textured fine sil-
ver foil; 1" × 1¼". Photograph, the artists.

Fig. 4-13 Jonah and the Whale, *1981. Audrey B. Komrad. Trans-*
parent cloisonné enamel on copper, gold and silver foil, ivory; 2½"
× 9½". Photograph, the artist.

The color inside the kiln will indicate firing temperatures:

dark red	approximately 1300°F(704°C)
becoming dark cherry red	1350°F–1450°F(732°C–788°C)
then bright cherry red	1450°F–1500°F(788°C–816°C)
takes on a yellow-red-orange color	1550°F–1600°F(843°C–871°C)
then more intense yellow-orange	over 1600°F(871°C)

Correcting warped enamels

When an enamel has been fired two or three times, the shape may
become warped. This can be corrected easily, but remember that the
metal is annealed and extremely soft, so great care is needed to prevent
further damage to the metal.

As soon as the enamel has been removed from the kiln, pick up the
piece with the kiln trowel and place it on a flat, heat-resistant surface.
The contact of the trowel with the enamel will chill the surface suf-
ficiently so the enamel will not stick to the trowel. If the trowel does
stick to the surface, there has probably been too much enamel applied.
The weight of the kiln trowel and the pressure of your gloved hand
are often the only weight necessary to correct the warping and straighten
the enamel project. Sometimes a commercial press-plate or a flatiron
can be used, but these weights tend to cool the edges of the enamel
too rapidly. The enamel project can be worked with at temperatures
between 1500°F–1000°F (816°C–538°C). Below 1000°F (538°C), touching
the enamel surface with a tool will often cause cracks.

Fig. 4-14 *The pressure of your hand and trowel is often the only weight necessary to correct warping. Trowel courtesy of Seaire Manufacturing.*

Fig. 4-15 *A commercial press-plate used to correct warping. Press plate courtesy of Seaire Manufacturing.*

Fig. 4-16 *A flatiron can be used to correct warping.* Note *trivet marks on enamel surface: these can be avoided by using the correct trivet.*

Cleaning and stoning between firings

During the many firings that a project will go through, the edges of the metal may become contaminated with excess enamel, or with firescale if copper is used. After each firing, the project edges should therefore be stoned. This process will become a good working habit; it takes only a few seconds and the results are well worth the extra effort.

If left, firescale on copper will contaminate the kiln on successive firings. Nothing is worse than removing a smooth white enamel from the kiln only to find small greenish-black flecks spread across the surface. Many valuable minutes will be spent trying to remove the specks from the enamel, and the firescale from the kiln.

Excessive drops of enamel that fire onto the edges of a project also need to be removed. On the following firing, they will become soft again and flow, perhaps dropping to the bottom of the kiln, or onto the trivet supporting the project. When this happens and the project is cool, the overflow of enamel will have to be broken away. This could damage the surface of the enamel. Any excess enamel that is fired onto a trivet can either be broken off with a hammer (protect your eyes), or filed away with a coarse file.

To stone the edges of the metal project, hold the cold enamel under running water and, with an Alundum stone held at right angles use a filing motion to remove just the discolored edge of the metal (Fig. 4-17). Methodically work around the edge, being careful not to remove any enamel from the face of the project.

Flush well with running water to remove the stoning residue. Check for missed areas, and repeat if necessary. Any overflow of enamel will be removed from the edges at the same time.

Fig. 4-17 *Stoning edges with an Alundum stone.*

Fig. 4-18 *Stoning the enamel surface with an Alundum stone.*

This procedure can be carried out with a coarse file (without water) instead of an Alundum stone. Filing may be a few seconds quicker, but extra care must be taken to ensure that the metal file does not chip the edges of the enamel surface. The project still needs to be washed after the filing, and you must be careful not to let the filings fall onto your worktable and contaminate your enamels.

Fig. 4-19 *Triangle 1, 1980. Pamela Harlow. Transparent and opalescent enamels over opaque white on copper enamel threads; matt surface; sandblasted plexiglas mount; 9″ × 5¼″. Photograph, Steve Young.*

Stoning or filing the metal edges is recommended after *every* firing. Taking care of the edges of the project is just another process in producing good work habits and good craftsmanship.

Sometimes it is necessary to stone the surface of a project: stoning the surface of an enamel is necessary when making a matt surface for underglaze pencils and crayons; when removing enamel from cloisonné wires; when leveling a finished cloisonné surface; when removing an area of color not to your liking; when removing contaminants that may have been fired into the surface; or when a flat finish is desirable.

Alundum, a vitrified white stone, is the superior stone to use for this process. It cuts quickly and does not leave a gray residue. If any of the powdered stone dust is left on the surface by error, it does not show when left in situ and fired.

Stoning should again be carried out under running water with the stone flat on the surface for all-over work. Small areas can be attended to with a corner of the stone. Again, rinse well and brush thoroughly with a fiberglass brush before continuing.

Peonies for Your Thoughts, 1982. Glenice Lesley Matthews. Silver cloisonné on fine silver; transparent and opalescent enamels set in sterling with moonstone, antique glass beads and fine silver Etruscan chain; pendant, 3" diameter. Photograph, Michael J. Oliver.

Urban Life: Apart-ment, 1981. Marian Slepian. Fine silver cloisonné on copper relief, mounted on Lucite; 24" x 48" (framed). Photograph, the artist.

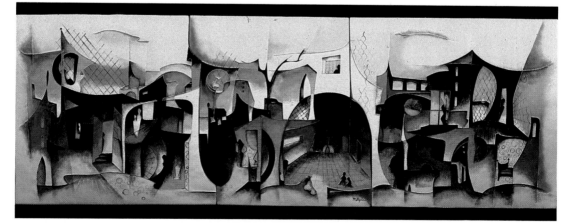

Pin, 1982. Martha Banyas.
Enamels on copper with
silver; 2" x 2½". Photograph,
the artist.

Pink Delilah. *Barbara Satterfield. Cloisonné enam-
el on copper; sterling silver,
glass, agate and rose quartz
beads; 2½" x 1¾". Photo-
graph, the artist.*

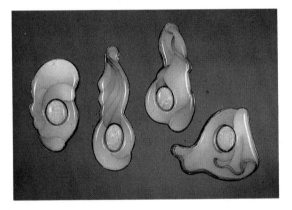

Pins, 1982. Connie Brauer.
14K, 20K and 24K gold with
opals; opalescent cloisonné;
1¾" x 1" each. Photograph,
the artist.

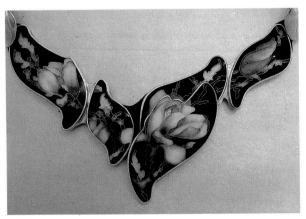

Magnolia Collar, 1982. *Merry
Lee and John Howell. Cloisonné enamels on silver;
forged and fabricated sterling setting; 7" wide. Photograph, John Howell.*

Tailed Moth, *1981. John Paul Miller. 18K gold with transparent enamels on pure gold granulation; 2¾" x 3". Photograph, the artist.*

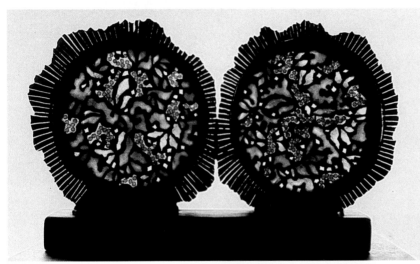

My Garden in August. *Kenneth Bates. Plique-à-jour enamel on mahogany stand; 8" x 5" Photograph, the artist.*

Lovers' Quilt Fragments, *1981. Pamela Harlow. Predominantly opaque enamels, wood frames; 5" x 5" each. (Left to right)* top row: *Prickly Pear, Hunger, Cherry Blossoms, The Cat;* center: *Bleeding Hearts, Burning, Night Highways, Snow Iris;* bottom: *Garden Paths, Jealousy, Eclipse, Window. Photograph, Steve Young.*

Neckpiece, 1980. Correen Kaufman. Cloisonné enamel, sterling silver setting. Photograph, the artist.

Brass Landscape. Fred Uhl Ball. Transparent enamels over brass; 4" x 6". Photograph, Bruce Beck.

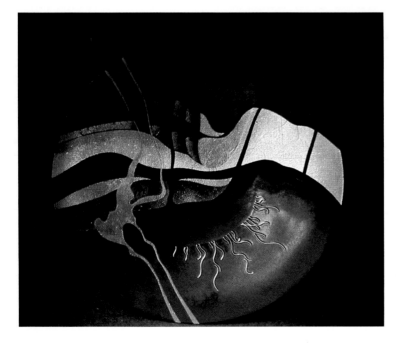

Parched Earth. Jenny Gore, South Australia. Enamels with fine silver and gold foil, fine silver wire, gold plated edge; 16½" diameter. Photograph, the artist.

Best Friends Series. *Shirley Rosenthal. High-fired opaque enamels, mounted on Plexiglas; 24" x 36". Photograph, the artist.*

Rosy Crucifixion, 1982. *David C. Freda. Wall sculpture, enamels on aluminum; fabrication of silver, brass, copper, leather thread, hummingbird, branch; 3" x 7" x 4". Photograph, the artist.*

Chapeau *detail, 1979. Patricia G. Telesco. Champlèvé enamel on hand-formed copper bowl; 10" x 9½" x 2" bowl. Photograph, Ray Stanyard.*

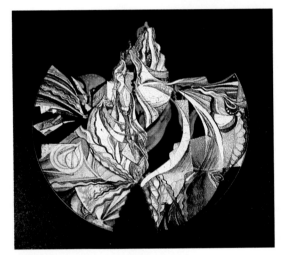

Untitled. *Harold B. Helwig. Limoges enamels, gold, silver foil, metallic oxides on copper. Photograph, the artist.*

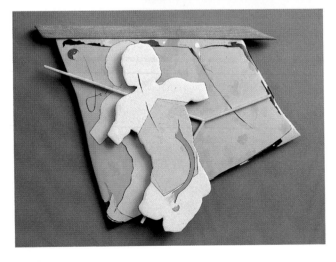

Figure with Fragment, 1982. *Jamie Bennett. Opaque enamels on copper; acrylic paint, wood; 6¾" x 8¼" x 1". Photograph, the artist.*

Vase. *Louis Comfort Tiffany.*
Enamel on copper; 14½" high.
Copyright © 1982 by The
Metropolitan Museum of Art;
Gift of William D. and Rose D.
Barker, 1981. (1981.444)

Bowl, 1982. *June Schwarcz.*
Enameled copper foil; elec-
troplated, iron plated; 6⅛"
high. Photograph, M. Lee
Fatherree.

Stick Pin Series, Bundle #1. *Glenice Lesley Matthews. Enamel on copper; gold, silver, fiber. Photograph, Michael J. Oliver.*

Paperweight. *Polly Rombold. Gold cloisonné enamel on fine silver, mounted on Lucite; 2½" x 3". Photograph, Michael J. Oliver.*

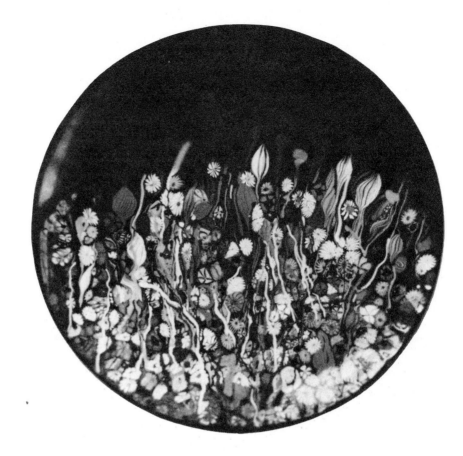

PART • TWO

Six projects
step by step

The six step-by-step projects in Chapters 5 through 10 were designed to give the inexperienced enamelist the necessary information on a variety of techniques. After completing the six projects, the enamelist's repertoire of skills should ensure success in the wide range of enameling techniques covered in Part Four: basse-taille, grisaille, plique-à-jour, and many others. The procedural instruction should also inspire the confidence to experiment and enjoy all the enameling methods.

Basic preparations are discussed in detail in Chapter 5, then condensed for ready reference in later project chapters, as a reminder to develop good work habits and a methodical approach to the preparation of the materials and metals.

Celebration, 1982. Estelle Schwartz. Stencils, sifting and Limoges on copper; 14″ × 14″. Photograph, the artist.

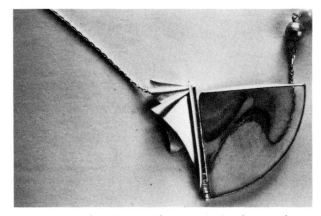

Kimono: From The River, To The Sea, 1980. Barbara Mail. Pendant, cloisonné enamel on copper, sterling silver setting, baroque and biwa pearls; 1¾″ × 2″ × ⅓″. Photograph, the artist.

Overleaf: Floral Garden. Janine Matthews. Floral lumps, cattail threads and transparent enamels on copper; 6″ diameter.

Fig. 5-1 Flint Hills Study #12. *Roxane Riva. Grass used for stencils; sifted opaque and transparent enamels on steel.*

·5·
Sgraffito and stencils

Sgraffito, the art term for scratching a decorative design onto a surface, and stencils are both easy, quick techniques for applying designs to enamel surfaces. Used in combination, they form the first technique of the six projects which serve as an introduction to enameling.

Inexperienced enamelists often encounter difficulty in controlling the quantity of enamel sifted onto the project surface; assessing the optimum deposit comes with experience. The sgraffito and stencil techniques will help to establish this criterion.

Fig. 5-2 *Supplies for the sgraffito and stencils project.*

Supplies

3-inch (76-mm) diameter, 18-gauge (1.024 mm) copper disc

Enamels:
counter enamel; two opaque enamels, one light and one dark

Scalex or similar

Binding agent (such as Klyr-Fire)

80-mesh sifter, large

2 large paintbrushes: a good quality #12 and an inexpensive #12

1 small paintbrush, #003

Scissors or X-acto knife

Stiff paper

Tape

Scribe

Step-by-step directions

Step 1. Cleaning the disc

Clean a 3-inch (76-mm) diameter, 18-gauge (1.024 mm) copper disc by placing it in a pickle bath for approximately 5 minutes, or until it is a clean pink color (see Chapter 3 for preparation of the pickle bath). Remove the disc from the bath with copper tongs (Fig. 5-3) and wash off the pickle under running water. Using your fingers as an applicator, apply powdered pumice to the surface of the metal (Fig. 5-4). Scrub vigorously, working methodically over both front and back surfaces. There will be less likelihood of pits in the enamel surface—and better results all around—if you take extra care during this stage. If you have trouble achieving a bright clean surface, scrub the metal with a fiber-

Fig. 5-3 *Remove disc from pickle with copper tongs.*

Fig. 5-4 *Apply pumice, then scrub disc vigorously with your fingers.*

Fig. 5-5 *If water draws up in a puddle as shown, the surface is not perfectly clean.*

Fig. 5-6 *When water lies in a sheet over the surface, the copper disc is clean and ready for enameling.*

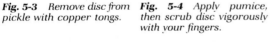
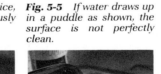
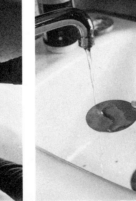

Fig. 5-7 *Always handle an enamel project by its bare edges.*

Fig. 5-8 *Applying an even coat of liquid firescale inhibitor.*

Fig. 5-9 *Apply an even coat of adhesive agent that has been diluted 50% with distilled water.*

glass brush, again working under running water. A final wipe with saliva helps to alkalize the surface of the copper. Baking soda can be used instead, but be careful not to leave a residue on the surface.

When the disc looks completely clean, it is possible to make a quick test for confirmation. Slowly run clean water onto the surface of the disc; if the water "draws up" and lies in puddles or beads (Fig. 5-5), oily residues are still present. If the water lies in a complete sheet over the surface (Fig. 5-6), the disc is clean and ready for enameling.

The cleaning process can often become frustrating at this point, when no amount of pumice treatment seems to produce the clean surface you need. It is sometimes necessary to start again, repickling the disc and proceeding as outlined above. If the surface of the copper is dark and greasy, annealing (see Chapter 3) can help rid the surface of contaminants. Once you have achieved the desired bright, clean color, take care not to contaminate the metal again by placing your fingers or other foreign objects on the surface. If you have oily skin, or have to wear protective creams or lotions, wear rubber gloves when handling the metal. Always support the disc by its edges (Fig. 5-7). Dry the disc with a lint-free linen cloth.

Some enamelists recommend using detergent and/or steel wool for cleaning. There is always the possibility that a detergent film will be left on the surface of the clean copper, invisible because of the wetting agents in the detergent. Steel wool particles are another hazard. If any particles are present when the enamel is fired, the steel wool fragments will fuse into the enamel surface, leaving black streaks which can only be removed with extra work. Although these alternatives are not recommended, as long as the artist achieves a perfectly clean surface on the copper, whatever works best for the individual can be used.

Step. 2 Applying firescale inhibitor

The next two steps should be completed immediately; if the clean copper disc is left for several hours, or overnight, the clean surface will start to oxidize and may interfere with excellent results. (If the

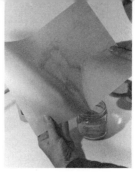

Fig. 5-10 *Place 80-mesh counter enamel into a large sifter.*

Fig. 5-11 *Control sifting by gently tapping the exterior of the sifter. Work around the edge of the disc first.*

Fig. 5-12 *Apply a smooth, even coat of 80-mesh enamel. Ultimate thickness should be approximately $\frac{1}{32}$" (0.7937mm).*

Fig. 5-13 *Return excess enamel to container.*

surface becomes contaminated in any way, or has been left for a period of time, repeat Step 1.)

Using an inexpensive #12 paintbrush, coat the front (image) side of the copper disc with a thick, even coat of liquid firescale inhibitor made from clay substances (Scalex or a similar product). See Fig. 5-8. Clean the brush under running water when the application is complete. Allow the Scalex-coated surface to dry. If a heat lamp is used, it will take 3 to 4 minutes; otherwise, let the Scalex air dry until the surface is flat and dull, which may take as long as 15 to 20 minutes, depending upon such weather conditions as humidity and temperature extremes.

Step 3. Counter enameling

When the Scalex is dry, turn the copper disc over and place it onto a ceramic trivet kept especially for this purpose; do not use a trivet which is to be used in the kiln. With a thoroughly clean, good quality #12 sable brush, carefully apply onto the bare (back) side an even coat of an adhesive agent or binder that has been diluted with 50% distilled water (Fig. 5-9). The adhesive can by Klyr-Fire, gum tragacanth, gum arabic, agar, or Thompson's Enamel Holding Agent. Klyr-Fire is a commercially manufactured binder which produces excellent results; gum arabic is a derivative of a species of acacia; gum tragacanth comes from a thorny plant; agar is derived from seaweed; Thompson's Enamel Holding Agent is a water-based binder. Any of these organic binders can be used successfully; again, the artist will find a personal preference. When applying the binder, make certain there are no air bubbles and that the binder covers the disc completely to the edges. If the binder "draws back" from the edges, it is an indication of a contaminated surface. It will be necessary to go back to the sink, wash off the binder and Scalex and repeat the entire cleaning procedure outlined in Step 1. Reapply the Scalex as in Step 2, allow to dry and continue.

NOTE: Applying the binder to small surfaces with a paintbrush is the recommended way. On large surfaces, such as bowls, an atomizer is more convenient and it is easier to get good coverage. Using an atomizer on small pieces tends to be wasteful and fills the air with excessive pollutants.

Immediately after application of the binder, using a large sifter, dust an even coat of 80-mesh counter enamel onto the wet surface (Fig. 5-10). Control of the sifting process is achieved by gently tapping the exterior of the sifter, which is held approximately 6 inches above the disc (Fig. 5-11). This technique allows for gentle dispersion of the enamel. Work around the outside edges first, before applying the enamel to the center section. Care should be taken not to pile up areas of sifted enamel. Sufficient enamel is applied when the bare copper is no longer visible through the sifted enamel coating. (Fig. 5-12) The correct thickness is approximately $\frac{1}{32}$ inch (0.7937 mm). When an uneven or lumpy buildup occurs, wash off the enamel and begin again. This will necessitate another coat of Scalex, which is water soluble and will have washed away with the enamel and the binder.

When applying counter enamel, place the disc on a ceramic trivet (kept especially for worktable procedures), a bottle cap or a coin, centered on a sheet of clean paper. This prop elevates the disc, making it easier to handle when it is moved from your worktable to the drying area of the kiln. The sheet of paper used under the disc collects excess enamel, which can be returned to the bottle for future use, providing it has not been contaminated with foreign matter or other colors (Fig. 5-13). Discard each sheet of paper after use.

Place the disc with the sifted enamel under a heat lamp and allow to dry for approximately 5 to 10 minutes. If a heat lamp is not available, placing the disc on top of the kiln will hasten the drying. However, if the kiln is used as a drying area, utmost care must be used when opening and closing the kiln door. Any vibration whatsoever will knock the drying enamel off the disc. Drying on top of the kiln is *not* recommended in classroom situations. The enamel can also be left to dry naturally, without heat aids. This may take 30 to 40 minutes, depending on weather conditions, and the type and amount of binder used. It is essential that the disc be *completely dry* before placing it into the kiln. If it is still damp from the binder, the enamel may pop off the surface when the heat from the kiln hits the wet surface of the disc.

Application of the counter enamel (or backing enamel) is necessary to equalize stress between the enamel and the metal, thus preventing the surface on the reverse side from cracking. When the front (image) side of an enamel piece is to have multiple layers of enamel, it is sometimes advisable to apply two coats of counter enamel to help eliminate stress caused by the extremes in the thickness of the enamel surfaces. Counter enamel is much less expensive and often has many colors mixed together; when it is fired, the effect is a "tweed" appearance. If the back of the piece will be seen (as in a bowl), you may prefer to use a complementary color, or the same color for both the front and the back of the piece.

Step 4. Firing the counter enamel

When the counter enamel is completely dry, place the disc carefully on a stainless steel trivet large enough so that *only the edges* of the disc touch the wings of the trivet. If the trivet does not have a recessed area for a kiln trowel (or kiln fork) to slip under, place the trivet and disc on a mesh firing rack. Gently place the trivet assemblage into the kiln, which has been preheated to 1500°F (816°C) with the kiln trowel or fork (Fig. 5-14). Protect yourself with long, heat-resistant gloves on your hands and the correct protective glasses for your eyes. It is advisable to wear long-sleeved, flame-resistant clothing as well.

Fire the enamel for approximately 2 minutes; as each firing may vary according to weather conditions, size of kiln, and size of work, it is advisable to take a quick peek into the kiln after about 1½ minutes. Do not open the door wide, as this will let out too much heat. Do not use the tiny opening in the kiln door as an observation hole; looking through it can damage your eyes, especially if you are wearing contact lenses.

The following stages can be observed as an enameled surface reaches maturity: after about 1½ minutes at 1400°–1500°F (760°–816°C) the en-

Fig. 5-14 *The enamel is placed in the preheated kiln.*

Fig. 5-15 *Example of an "orange peel" surface when an enamel is not fired to maturity.*

amel will turn black and its granular quality will be quite apparent; a short time later it will begin to glow slightly and have an "orange-peel" appearance (Fig. 5-15). A few seconds later, the piece will take on a soft red glow from its inner heat and the enamel will have a shiny, liquid appearance. At this point, the enamel is fired to maturity and is ready to be taken from the kiln.

Remove the enamel/trivet assemblage from the kiln with the trowel, protecting yourself again with gloves and glasses. If the surface still has an orange-peel effect, it can be returned immediately to the kiln and refired for 30 seconds or so longer. If the orange-peel is not too craterous, it can be ignored because the surface will correct itself when the next coat is fired.

If, upon removal from the kiln, the enamel surface has pulled away from the edges of the disc, the piece may have been overfired. When this happens, the enamel is burnt away, leaving bare exposed copper. (See troubleshooting section, page 129, for correcting this problem, or when pinholes or pits are evident).

Place the hot trivet assemblage onto a heat-resistant surface, away from unfired work in an area devoid of drafts. This is a courtesy to your fellow workers, as well as protection for your own work. While the enameled disc is cooling, firescale (flaking black copper oxide) from the edges of the enameled disc may fly off the surface, fill the air and contaminate other unfired pieces in the vicinity. The firescale causes unsightly spots and pits when fired on an enamel surface. A hot enamel which cools too rapidly because of the sudden changes in the temperature often crazes or flakes off the copper surface. When the enamel is applied too thickly, the same defect may occur.

It is advisable for inexperienced enamelists to practice picking up the trivet assemblage with the kiln trowel or fork and placing it down again gently. Placing the assemblage into a kiln tends to take more time than expected and, while the kiln door is open, the temperature drops; it is then necessary to fire the enamel for a longer period of time at a lower temperature. Aim to have the kiln door open for the least possible time, thus maintaining an even temperature inside.

Step 5. Pickling the counter enamel

When the metal cools, the Scalex on the front of the disc will flake off, leaving a relatively clean surface (Fig. 5-16). The purpose of the Scalex is to protect your piece from excessive firescale buildup and the deposit of that firescale onto other work, or onto the inside of the kiln. When firescale is present inside a kiln, it will float around during future firings and may be deposited on the surface of your project. Firescale should be eliminated at all cost.

When the counter-enameled disc is cold to the touch (about 10 to 15 minutes), return your project to the pickle bath for approximately

5 minutes and proceed with cleaning the bare copper surface as de-scribed in Step 1. The working, or front side, of the disc is now ready for the application of enamel. The counter-enameled surface should be thoroughly neutralized with pumice and baking soda after being exposed to the pickle bath. Flush the surface to remove all residue.

NOTE: This is the only time an enameled piece (unless it is lead-free, acid-resistant enamel) is put into the pickle bath. If left in the pickle bath for any length of time, the acid will attack the previously fired enamel surface, causing it to break down.

Step 6. Sifting the first enamel coat

Place the freshly prepared disc, bare metal side up, on a ceramic trivet or elevator. A clean sheet of paper for enamel collection should be centered underneath the elevated disc. To the clean copper surface, apply an even coat of diluted binder as described in Step 3. Care should be taken to observe the binder's characteristics: if it "draws back," additional cleaning of the metal is required.

Immediately after the binder is applied, sift onto the wet surface an even coat of 80-mesh white enamel (or selected opaque color) that

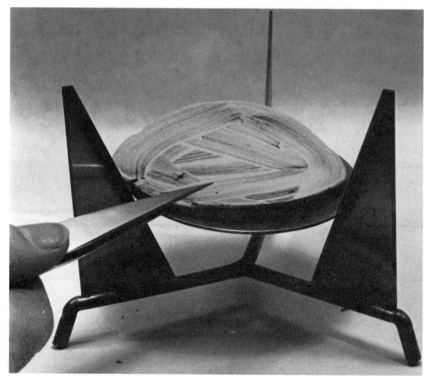

Fig. 5-16 *After firing, the firescale inhibitor will flake off, leaving a relatively clean surface.*

has been previously placed in a large sifter. Again, control the sifting process by gently tapping the exterior of the sifter, which should be held approximately 6 inches above the disc. Care should be taken not to pile up areas of sifted enamel.

Step 7. Firing the first coat

Place the disc with the sifted enamel under the heat lamp to dry. It should take approximately 5 to 10 minutes. Carefully reposition the disc onto the kiln furniture assemblage and place in the kiln at a temperature of 1500°F (816°C) for approximately 2 minutes. Care should be taken not to over-fire whites, as they tend to burn out and leave a greenish-black copper oxide cast to the surface, particularly around the edges. The following stages can be observed as an enameled surface reaches maturity: after about $1\frac{1}{2}$ minutes at 1400°–1500°F (760°–816°C), the enamel will turn black and its granular quality will be quite apparent; a short time later it will begin to glow slightly and take on an "orange-peel" texture. Finally, a few seconds later, the piece will take on a soft red glow from its inner heat, and the enamel will have a shiny, liquid appearance. At this point, the enamel is fired to maturity and is ready to be taken from the kiln. Observing the courtesy rules, remove the disc assemblage from the kiln and cool in a draft-free environment.

Whites and some opaques are not the best enamels for coverage; it is usually necessary to apply a second coat of white enamel to achieve a good even surface on which to work. (If pinholes or other problems appear, refer to the trouble-shooting section in chapter 12.)

Step 8. Stoning the edges

Now that both sides of the copper disc have been fired, it is no longer advisable to pickle the disc to clean the exposed edges which develop a black firescale coating during each firing. To eliminate firescale, the edges are stoned with an Alundum stone under running water. Hold the disc at right angles to the stone as shown in Figure 5-17, and remove only the black firescale, leaving the edges bright and clean. Care should be taken not to stone away the enamel. Flush well with clean water, making sure no stoning residue remains.

This stoning process is recommended after *every* firing. Taking care of the edges of your enamel pieces is an important process in producing good work habits and good craftsmanship.

Firescale on the edges of an enamel piece can also be removed by filing with a #2 file, but utmost care must be taken not to chip the enamel from the surface. For correct filing procedures, refer to page 49.

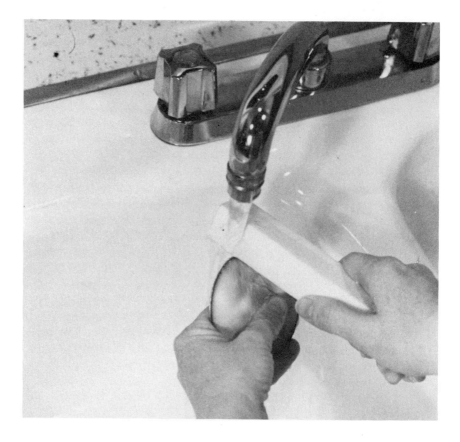

Step 9. Stenciling and sgraffito designing

The disc is now ready for the creative part of your project. To save time it is an excellent idea to have created your design and cut out the stencil while waiting for the disc to dry or cool during the previous steps.

There are two types of stencils that can be used:

1. A positive stencil, which will produce a negative pattern (Fig. 5-18).

2. A negative stencil, which will produce a positive pattern (Figs. 5-19 and 5-20).

Cut out the design. If a negative stencil is chosen, care should be taken not to cut through the surrounding edges. A matt (or X-acto) knife is a useful tool for this process. Add finger tabs made from tape to the stencil; these aid in the removal of the stencil from the surface of the enamel after it has been used.

Choose an 80-mesh enamel in a contrasting color to the background shade and place in sifter ready for use. Cover the fired enamel surface with diluted binder; then place the stencil in the required position.

Fig. 5-18 *A positive stencil, which will produce a negative pattern.*

Fig. 5-19 *A negative stencil, which will produce a positive pattern.*

Fig. 5-20 *The sifted enamel images produced by the negative/ positive and the positive/negative stencils.*

Fig. 5-21 *Place the stencil, with added tabs, onto the enameled surface which has been coated with diluted binder. Sift on 80-mesh enamel.*

Fig. 5-22 *Carefully remove the stencil from the still-damp surface.*

Fig. 5-23 *Use a fine paintbrush to remove excess granules of enamel.*

Fig. 5-24 *Scratch through the dry, unfired enamel to create the sgraffito design.*

Fig. 5-25 *Continuing to refine the design.*

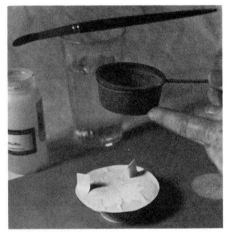

The binder helps to keep the stencil in place (Fig. 5-21). Dust enamel over the surface, making sure there is no buildup in some areas, and that it is just thick enough for even coverage without any of the background color showing through.

Carefully remove the stencil from the still-damp surface of the disc (Fig. 5-22). This should be done without disturbing the dusted enamel at the edges of the design. If the edges are disturbed, use a fine paintbrush dampened with a little water to carefully pick up the excess granules of enamel (Fig. 5-23).

Allow the stenciled surface to dry under the heat lamp, then return the disc to your work area. With a scribe, a toothpick, straight pin, or jeweler's tool, scratch through the dried, unfired enamel to create the

Fig. 5-26 Flow Chart #1, detail. Thomas J. Terceira. Cloisonné on copper, with opaque showing breakthrough. Photograph, Anthony C. Terceira.

sgraffito design (Fig. 5-24). Again, use a fine paintbrush dampened with a little water to carefully pick up any unwanted enamel granules.

Step 10. Firing the stenciled enamel

Place the disc on the kiln furniture and fire in the kiln, as described in Step 4, for approximately $1\frac{1}{2}$ minutes at 1500°F (816°C). Careful timing is important with this firing. If the enamel disc is fired too long, or too hot, the background enamel color may start to float to the surface while the stencil color sinks. This gives a spotted or mottled appearance. This effect is not necessarily undesirable—many artistic effects can result from this type of over-firing (Fig. 5-26). By combining soft-fusing enamels over medium-fusing enamels, or vice versa, a similar effect can be achieved with more control.

Fig. 5-28 She Brushed off Her Fringe of Waving Grass. *Glenice Lesley Matthews. Transparent and opaque enamels on copper; torn paper towel stencils, sifted enamels, pewter container; 4" diameter, $2\frac{1}{2}$" high.*

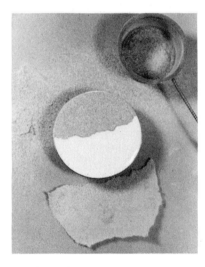

Fig. 5-27 *The sifted enamel image from a torn paper towel used as a stencil.*

Finishing and stenciling alternatives

Additional stenciling or sgraffito work can be incorporated into the project in subsequent firings. When satisfied with the result, stone edges, and finish as instructed in Chapter 11.

Since this is the first project, it is advisable to keep the imagery simple. When cutting the stencil, keep the lines broad and uncomplicated. Look to Miro, Arp and Picasso for inspiration.

A torn paper towel can be used as a stencil for mountains, clouds and organic imagery (Figs. 5-27 and 5-28). Found objects, such as leaves, lace, and grasses also can be used as stencils (Fig. 5-28). Creative imagery can come from many sources.

Soft-edged stencils can be created by holding the stencil a few inches from the background surface. When the enamel is sifted over the area, the edges of the stencil will be soft and undefined.

Throughout this and every project, notes should be kept on colors used, firing temperatures, firing times, difficulties encountered, and so on. Add comments to the notes about the finished project's appearance, your personal satisfaction and/or frustrations, ideas and alternatives for next time, effects, and ambitions.

Fig. 6-1 *Wet inlay box. Carol Adams. Wet inlay enamels on copper with plaited rayon. Photograph, Robert Fuston Hall.*

·6·
Wet packing

A controlled application of a design onto the enamel surface can be achieved with the wet packing technique. A series of colors can be placed next to each other, without bleeding one color into another. Colors can be blended, or shaded, but it is an optical blending rather than a physical mixing of the colors.

Mastering the wet packing technique gives an enamlist great dexterity. Used in conjunction with other techniques, it is a most useful tool. The wet packing process is used again extensively for the sixth project, in combination with cloisonné, in Chapter 10.

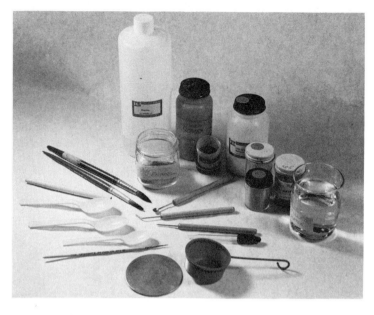

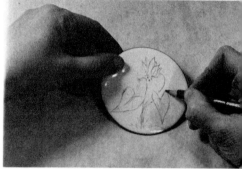

Fig. 6-2 *Supplies for the wet inlay project.*

Fig. 6-3 *An 8008 Stabilo pencil will mark directly onto an enamel surface, and will fire out.*

Supplies

3-inch (76 mm) diameter, 18-gauge (1.024 mm) copper disc
Enamels:
  counter enamel; one background opaque; two to four contrasting opaque colors for the design
Plastic spoons (or mixing tray)
Set of inlay tools

Two eyedroppers: one for the binder, one for distilled water
Scalex or similar
Binding agent (Klyr-Fire or similar)
Distilled water
80-mesh sifter
Paintbrushes
Stabilo 8008 pencil

Step-by-step directions

Step 1. Pickling and cleaning the disc

See Chapter 5, Step 1, and Figs. 5-1 through 5-7.

Clean a 3-inch (76 mm), 18-gauge (1.024 mm) copper disc by placing it in a pickle bath for approximately five minutes, or until it is a clean pink color. Remove the disc from the bath with copper tongs and wash off the pickle under running water.

Using your fingers as an applicator, apply powdered pumice to the surface of the metal. Scrub vigorously, working methodically over both the front and back surfaces. When a bright clean surface is achieved, give the copper disc a final wipe with saliva, which acts as a neutralizer. Give the disc the water test for cleanliness.

Step 2. Applying firescale inhibitor

See Chapter 5, Step 2, and Fig. 5-8.

Using a large, inexpensive paintbrush (#12), coat the front (imagery) side of the copper disc with a thick, even coat of liquid firescale inhibitor (Scalex or a similar product). Clean the brush under running water when the application is complete. Allow the Scalex-coated surface to dry. If a heat lamp is used, it will take 3 to 4 minutes; otherwise let the Scalex air-dry until the surface is flat and dull.

Step 3. Counter enameling

See Chapter 5, step 3, and Figs. 5-9 through 5-13.

When the Scalex is dry, turn the copper disc over, place it on a ceramic trivet (kept especially for this purpose) and carefully apply onto the bare (back) side an even coat of binder that has been dilluted 50% with distilled water. When applying the binder, make certain there are no air bubbles and that the binder covers the disc completely to the edges. If the binder "draws back," the surface is contaminated and it is necessary to repeat Steps 1 and 2 before continuing.

While the binder is still wet, sift an even coat of 80-mesh counter enamel onto the surface. Sufficient enamel should be applied so that the bare copper is no longer visible through the sifted enamel coating. Place the disc with the sifted enamel under the heat lamp and allow to dry. A quick check on the drying process is to touch the underside of the disc with your finger. If the disc is warm to the touch, the binder should be dry.

Step 4. Firing the counter enamel

See Chapter 5, step 4, and Figs. 5-14 through 5-17.

When the counter enamel is completely dry, place the disc carefully on a stainless steel trivet large enough that only the edges of the disc touch the wings of the trivet. If the trivet does not have a recessed area for a kiln trowel or fork to slip under, place the trivet and disc on a mesh firing rack; the assemblage is now ready to place in the kiln. Place the assemblage into the kiln, protecting yourself with the recommended safety equipment, and fire the disc for approximately 2 minutes at 1500°F (816°C). After $1\frac{1}{2}$ minutes, check the process. When the enamel is fired to maturity, remove the assemblage from the kiln and allow to cool in a draft-free environment away from other enamels.

When the disc is cold to the touch, remove the Scalex coating and discard. Return your project to the pickle bath for approximately 5 minutes and proceed with the cleaning of the bare copper surface, using the recommended cleaning aids. The working, or front, side of the disc is now ready for the application of enamel. The counter enamel surface should be thoroughly neutralized after being exposed to the pickle bath.

Step 5. Applying and firing the background enamel

To the clean copper surface, apply an even coat of binder that has been diluted 50% with distilled water. (Check for "draw back" characteristics.) Sift onto the surface a coat of 80-mesh enamel in your selected color. Observe all application characteristics.

Allow the unfired enamel to dry under a heat lamp. Position the disc on a trivet assemblage, and fire in the kiln for approximately 2 minutes at 1500°F (816°C) (see page 63 for full procedure). Observing the courtesy rules, allow the enamel to cool in a draft-free environment. It may be necessary to apply a second coat of your chosen background color. If pits or holes occur, refer to the troubleshooting section in Chapter 13.

When the desired background coating has been achieved, stone the edges of the disc, flush with running water and proceed as follows.

Step 6. Designing for wet packing

Select a design to be transferred onto the enameled disc. Depending on your creative ability, you may choose to work spontaneously upon the enamel surface, or to transfer a design from your sketchbook. An 8008 Stabilo pencil or water soluble marker can be used directly upon the enamel surface (Fig. 6-3). Alternatively, a carbon-type paper which has no graphite or oil deposits can be successfully used to trace a design from your sketchbook onto the enamel surface. When fired, the transfer-paper imagery, which is biodegradable, disappears and should not promote holes or pits.

Select the colors for your design. Opaques are recommended for this project, although transparent enamel can be combined with the opaques to achieve a variety of effects. If you choose a transparent, remember that the color of the enameled disc will reflect through the transparent enamel and change the color of the transparent; e.g., red transparent over a white background will tend to look pink.

Use plastic spoons or a ceramic watercolor tray as mixing bowls. Do not use metal spoons, as the enamel may grind small metallic flakes off the spoon; when incorporated into the enamel mixture, these flakes will appear as dark specks or pits in the fired enamel. Fill the mixing container with a small quantity of enamel (remember, a little enamel goes a long way). Add to this enamel one or two drops of binder (Fig. 6-5) and enough drops of distilled water to make a thick paste, about the consistency of toothpaste. Mix carefully, try not to create bubbles, and leave for a few minutes to let the mixture permeate and settle (Fig. 6-7). If you add too much water, remove the excess liquid with the edge of a paper towel (Fig. 6-8). During use, the liquid

Fig. 6-4 *Fill the mixing container with a small quantity of enamel.*

Fig. 6-5 *Add one or two drops of binder.*

Fig. 6-6 *Add enough distilled water to make a paste.*

Fig. 6-7 *Mix carefully, trying not to create bubbles.*

enamel mixture may dry up; it is still usable and can be reactivated by adding a few drops of distilled water.

With a water-soluble marker, record on the handle of the plastic spoon the color number and name, e.g., "T207, Sky." This helps you to remember which color is in which spoon. After the enamels have been fired, they are quite often a different color from the unfired mixture. When working with many colors, it can become confusing.

Step 7. Applying wet enamels

Scoop up a small quantity of the enamel mixture with the wet inlay spatula (Fig. 6-11). Then, with the wet inlay applicator, carefully lay down the enamel mixture in the desired pattern (Fig. 6-12). The enamel should hold its shape; if it spreads out over the fired enamel surface in a puddle, there is too much water in the mixture. When this occurs, excess water should be blotted out of the mixing container. Using the old watercolor technique of capilliary action, a damp paintbrush will absorb the excess moisture from the mixture already applied to the design. An absorbent paper towel can also be used to draw out excess moisture (Fig. 6-13). Try to keep the application of the enamel smooth and even. Use the applicator to flatten out bumps and to puncture

Fig. 6-8 *Draw up excess liquid with the edge of a paper towel.*

Fig. 6-9 *Record the name and number of each enamel used.*

Fig. 6-10 *Enamels in plastic spoons and mixing tray ready to use.*

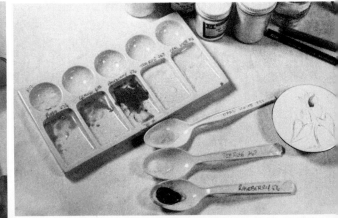

Fig. 6-11 *Scoop up a small quantity of enamel in a wet inlay spatula.*

any air bubbles. The applied enamel can also be smoothed by gently tapping the side of the disc with a paintbrush. The vibration created by the tapping will level the granules. Do not get too enthusiastic, or you will blur the edges of the design. Do not build up the enamel more than two or three grains high. Too thick an application will cause cracks and craters in the design when it is fired.

Keeping each color at a paste consistency, color after color can be juxtaposed onto the surface of the design without any "bleeding" of one color into another.

The metal inlay applicator does not suit everyone's technique for wet packing. Small sable-hair paintbrushes can be used quite successfully in place of this tool (Fig. 6-14). When using a paintbrush dab the enamel onto the surface, rather than using painterly brushstrokes. The natural characteristics of 80-mesh enamel do not lend themselves well to traditional painting techniques.

NOTE: With 80-mesh enamels it is *not* possible to mix new shades of color. Each minute grain of enamel retains its own color and, when fired, remains as a small speck of that color; e.g., red and white mixed together will not produce pink, but rather minute spots of red and white. Any appearance of pink comes from the optical mixing of the red and white grains in the retina of your eye. This phenomenon can be used to your advantage. For example, several shades of green can be gradually blended together to give the mottled appearance of leaves and other natural forms. To feather or blend two colors together, the

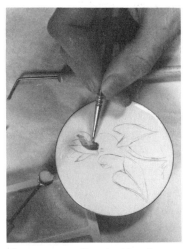

Fig. 6-12 *Apply the enamel with a wet inlay applicator, using a dapping motion.*

Fig. 6-13 *A paper towel will remove excess water from the design.*

Fig. 6-14 *Small artists' brushes can also be used as applicators.*

enamel mixture should be a little wetter to help you manipulate the enamel granules.

Step 8. Firing the enamel

Place the completed design under a heat lamp and allow to dry for 10 to 15 minutes. The recommended drying time is extended here because the water and binder have been mixed into the enamel. Consequently, each granule of enamel is *covered* with moisture, instead of just lying on the moisture, as with the sifted applications. Carefully place the disc onto a trivet assemblage and fire in the preheated kiln at 1500°F (816°C) for approximately 2 minutes.

Remove the enamel assemblage from the kiln, and observing the courtesy rules, allow the enamel to cool in a draft-free environment.

Additional wet packing and finishing

Additional wet packing can be added with repetitive firings until the desired design is achieved. Remember to stone the firescale from the edges after each firing.

When the design works to your satisfaction, stone the edges once again and finish as instructed in Chapter 12. Bring your sketchbook up-to-date with all firing procedures, colors used, and other useful data for future reference.

The enamel/binder mixture in the spoon can be kept for several days, so long as it is stored in a dust-free environment. The liquids dry up, but the mixture can be reactivated by simply adding a few

Fig. 6-15 Cyclamen. *Glenice Lesley Matthews. Wet inlay, transparents and opaques on copper; 12" diameter.*

drops of distilled water. This is another reason for marking your spoons with the enamel color and number. If the spoons are left for a few days, it is often difficult to remember which color is which. It is not advisable to keep the mixed enamels for extended periods, as the enamels will deteriorate.

Fig. 7-1 Tacky Threads Series. *Thomas S. Farrell. Opaque enamel on copper with threads, sterling silver setting; $1\frac{1}{2}'' \times 1\frac{1}{2}'' \times \frac{1}{4}''$. Photograph, V. Pipone.*

·7·
Threads and blobs or, "just for fun"

Threads and blobs should be approached as a spontaneous creative project. After the precise techniques of the first two projects, this short diversion should help increase the enjoyment of enameling. The technique of preparing the copper disc will become routine, leaving more time for creative thoughts.

Threads and lump enamel traditionally have been used for scrolling techniques. In this project, the preformed shapes of the lumps and threads are used to make the designs, taking full advantage of these characteristics.

Fig. 7-2 *Supplies for threads and blobs project.*

Supplies

3-inch (76 mm) diameter, 18-gauge (1.024 mm)
　　copper disc
Enamels:
　　counter enamel, background color, opaque
　　　　threads, opaque and transparent lumps

Binding agent
Needlenose tweezers
Scalex or similar
Paintbrushes
Spontaneity

Step-by-step directions

Step 1. Preparing the disc

See Chapter 5, steps 1 and 2, and Figs. 5-1 through 5-8.

Clean a 3-inch (76 mm), 18-gauge (1.024 mm) copper disc by placing it in a pickle bath for approximately 5 minutes, or until it is a clean, pink color. Remove the disc from the bath with copper tongs and wash off the pickle under running water.

Using your fingers as an applicator, apply powdered pumice to the surface of the metal. Scrub vigorously, working methodically over both front and back surfaces. When a bright, clean surface is achieved, give the copper disc a final wipe with saliva to neutralize the surface. Give the disc the water test for cleanliness.

Coat the front (image) side of the copper disc with a thick, even coat of liquid firescale inhibitor (Scalex or a similar product), using a #12 brush. Clean the brush under running water when the application is complete. Allow the Scalex-coated surface to dry. If a heat lamp is used, it will take 3 to 4 minutes; otherwise let the Scalex air-dry until the surface is flat and dull.

Step 2. Applying and firing the counter enamel

See Chapter 5, steps 3 and 4, and Figs. 5-9 through 5-17.

When the Scalex is dry, turn the copper disc over, place it on a ceramic trivet (kept especially for this purpose) and carefully apply onto the bare (back) side an even coat of binder that has been diluted 50% with distilled water. When applying the binder, make certain there are no air bubbles and that the binder covers the disc completely to the edges. If the binder "draws back," it is necessary to repeat Steps 1 and 2 before continuing with the procedures.

While the binder is still wet, sift an even coat of 80-mesh counter enamel onto the surface. Sufficient enamel should be applied so that the bare copper is no longer visible through the sifted enamel coating. Place the disc with the sifted enamel under the heat lamp and allow to dry.

When the counter enamel is completely dry, place the disc carefully on a stainless steel trivet and mesh firing rack. Place the assemblage into the kiln, protecting yourself with the recommended safety equipment, and fire the disc for approximately 2 minutes at 1500°F (816°C). After $1\frac{1}{2}$ minutes, check the firing process. When the enamel is fired to maturity, remove the assemblage from the kiln, using the correct equipment, and allow to cool in a draft-free environment away from other unfired enamels.

Step 3. Applying and firing the base coat

When the disc is cold to the touch, remove the Scalex coating and discard. Return your project to the pickle bath for approximately 5 minutes and proceed with the cleaning of the bare copper surface as described in Step 1. The working, or front, side of the disc is now ready for the application of the background enamel. The counter-enameled surface should be thoroughly neutralized after being exposed to the pickle bath.

To the clean copper surface, apply an even coat of the diluted binder, checking for "draw back" characteristics. Sift onto the surface an even coat of 80-mesh enamel in your selected color. You might try using a white opaque enamel.

Allow the unfired enamel to dry under the heat lamp. Position the disc on a trivet assemblage and fire in the preheated kiln for approximately 2 minutes at 1500°F (816°C). Observing the courtesy rules, allow the piece to cool in a draft-free environment. It may be necessary to apply a second coat of background enamel. Do not forget to stone the edges after every firing. If pits or holes occur, refer to the troubleshooting section in Chapter 12.

When the desired background coating has been achieved, stone the edges of the disc, flush with running water, and proceed as follows.

Step 4. Designing with threads and lumps

Empty container of enamel into a flat container or onto a clean sheet of white paper; do likewise with the lumps on another clean sheet of white paper. Pour a little binding agent into a shallow dish (Fig. 7-3).

Fig. 7-3 *Place lumps and threads on flat containers. Pour binder into a shallow dish.*

Using a pair of needlenose tweezers, select a thread, maybe for its shape or color, and dip the thread into the binding agent (Fig. 7-4). Place the coated thread in position on the enameled disc (Fig. 7-5).

Using this technique, continue working with the threads to build up a linear pattern. To counter-balance the linear design, introduce the enamel lumps, again dipping them in binder before placing on the enameled disc (Fig. 7-6). Keep the lumps small, the size of a grain of rice. A lump will take longer to melt and tends to keep its original shape unless fired at a higher temperature for a longer period of time. The lumps will "gather" into a natural round shape at higher temperatures.

Pleasing effects can be obtained by leaving the lumps as relief patterns on the fired surfaces. The threads can be placed one on top of the other and interwoven (Fig. 7-7). After firing, the threads will all have been incorporated into the same surface plane.

Fig. 7-4 *Dip selected thread into binder.*

Fig. 7-5 *Place binder-coated thread onto enamel surface in position.*

Fig. 7-6 *Add selected lumps to the enamel surface.*

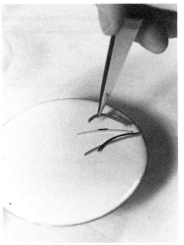

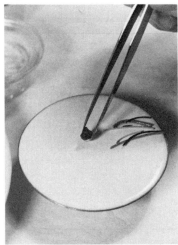

Fig. 7-7 *Interweave the threads and lumps.*

Fig. 7-8 *Fired thread design. Glenice Lesley Matthews. Opaque enamels and threads on copper; $2\frac{1}{2}''$ diameter.*

Step 5. Firing the design

The binder and lump/thread arrangement must be thoroughly dried before firing. A heat lamp will accelerate the drying time. Very carefully place the disc onto the trivet assemblage. Using the correct safety equipment, fire the disc at 1500°F (816°C) for approximately 2 minutes. Extra firing time may be needed for this procedure, depending upon the size of the lumps. Alternatively, the disc could be fired at a higher temperature (1650°F [898°C]) for a scant $1\frac{1}{2}$ minutes. If either of the latter methods is used, extreme care must be taken not to burn out the background enamel.

When the lump and thread enamels have matured, remove the disc assemblage from the kiln, observing all safety precautions and courtesy rules. Allow to cool in a draft-free environment.

Additional firings and finishing

Additional threads and lumps can be added, and the enamel project fired after each addition, although the threads will tend to spread and lose their linear quality.

Stone the firescale from the edges of the disc after each firing, and once again upon completion of the disc. For final finishing procedures, see Chapter 12.

Bring your sketchbook up-to-date. This project was designed to stimulate spontaneity and for enjoyment. Creative abstracts frequently become complex and beautiful designs.

Fig. 7-9 Commercial enamel threads and blobs available in many shapes. Supplies courtesy of Seaire Manufacturing.

Fig. 8-1 Brass Bed on a Persian Carpet. *Ruth Markus. Sculpture, Limoges enameling on fine silver, copper, brass and sterling silver; 12" × 8" × 6". Courtesy of the Spring Street Enamels Gallery.*

·8·
Limoges (painting) technique

Taking its name from the southern French town of Limoges, this painting technique has many applications. While it is possible to use 80-mesh enamels, much finer and more painterly work can be achieved with special painting enamels. This painting enamel can be made by grinding lump or large-mesh enamel to a fine powder with a mortar and pestle; bought ready-ground in a painting kit; or reclaimed by sifting from the 80-mesh enamels you have on hand. (This powdered enamel should not be confused with stains and oxides, described on page 159.)

For this technique, the powdered enamel must be combined with an oil- or water-based medium and mixed to a paste consistency (similar to oil paint) for use.

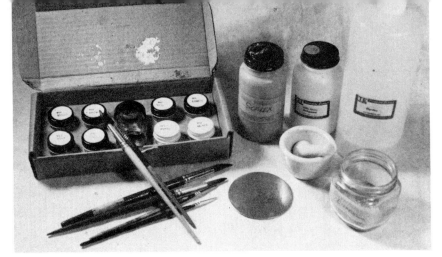

Fig. 8-2 *Supplies for the Limoges technique of enamel painting.*

Supplies

3-inch (76 mm) diameter, 18-gauge (1.024 mm) copper disc

Enamels:

counter enamel, opaque background color, selected shades of painting enamel

Mixing medium:

oil of lavender, oil of clove, or #5 thinning oil

Binder or water-based binder (Klyr-Fire or similar)

Scalex or similar

Mortar and pestle or sheet of glass

Paintbrushes, including #000

Sifters:

Standard 80-mesh

100/200/325-mesh sifting set (optional)

Fig. 8-3 *Painting kit.*

Fig. 8-4 *Rework painting enamels with mortar and pestle to remove any compacted masses.*

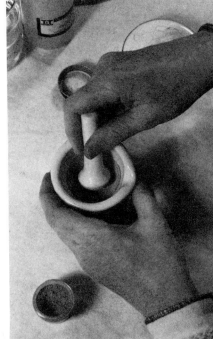

Preparation of painting enamels

Ready-ground enamel

These enamels can be bought from the supplier in a kit form, containing eight ½-ounce bottles of color and a 1-ounce bottle of squeegee oil (Fig. 8-3).

When using these ready-ground colors, it is often necessary to rework the powdered enamel in a mortar and pestle for a short time to eliminate any compact masses (Fig. 8-4). Working the ground enamel through a fine sifter will also rid the powder of these compacted masses. If these aggregates are allowed to remain, when the enamel is applied and fired, these masses will appear different from the rest of the painted areas—showing up either as lumps or as different colors.

Remove the squeegee oil from the kit. This oil is only usable when applying these painting enamels by the silkscreen techniques; at this stage of your enameling development, the squeegee oil can do more harm than good.

Screen preparation of 80-mesh enamel

The "fines" of 80-mesh enamels can be used for painting. This grading technique is particularly useful when several shades of one color are required. Each mesh size will give a slight variation in shade.

The easiest method of reclaiming the "fines" is to place five sifters, one inside the other. On the bottom, use a 325-mesh sifter, followed by a 200-mesh sifter, a 100-mesh sifter, an 80-mesh sifter, then a 60-mesh sifter on top. A catch pan is placed under the 325-mesh sifter.

Empty a quantity of 80-mesh enamel of your selected color into the top sifter. Place one or two large lumps of enamel in each sifter to help speed up the action of the enamels passing through the various sized meshes. Gently tapping the side of the stacked sifters will cause the enamel to fall through the screens according to particle size. This may take several minutes to complete, but it is worthwhile.

Eventually, you will have five or six grades of enamel: greater than 60 mesh, 60 mesh, 80 mesh, 100 mesh, 200 mesh and 325 mesh. The 325 mesh will be gathered in the collecting pan underneath (Fig. 8-6) and is ideal for the painting techniques. It will also include the "fines" which have a particle size smaller than 400 mesh. This is what we would normally wash away when washing enmel. Bottle these enamels according to particle size and mark accordingly. The 80-mesh or larger-mesh enamels are now in excellent condition, they require little or no washing and the transparent enamels are especially transparent.

This sifting method is an excellent alternative to washing the enamels, which was discussed in Chapter 2.

Fig. 8-5 *Sift enamel through graduated mesh screens to obtain painting grades of enamel.*

Fig. 8-6 *Six grades of enamel (from top left corner): greater than 60 mesh, 60 mesh, 80 mesh; second row, 100 mesh, 200 mesh, 325 mesh to infinity.*

Grinding painting enamel from lumps

Painting enamel can also be ground from lumps, using a mortar and pestle. This is a long and laborious method of obtaining an enamel for painting, especially when the sifting method or ready-prepared enamels work so well and more quickly.

Step-by-step directions

Step 1. Preparing the disc

See chapter 5, steps 1 and 2.

Clean a 3-inch (76 mm), 18-gauge (1.024 mm) copper disc by placing it in a pickle bath for approximately 5 minutes, or until it is a clean, pink color. Remove the disc from the bath with copper tongs and wash off the pickle under running water.

Using your fingers as an applicator, apply powdered pumice to the surface of the metal. Scrub vigorously, working methodically over both front and back surfaces. When a bright clean surface is achieved, give the copper disc a final wipe with saliva to neutralize the surface. Give the disc the water test for cleanliness.

Coat the front (image) side of the copper disc with a thick, even coat of liquid firescale inhibitor (Scalex or similar product). Clean the brush under running water when the application is complete. Allow the Scalex-coated surface to dry. If a heat lamp is used, it will take 3 to 4 minutes; otherwise, let the Scalex air-dry until the surface is flat and dull.

Step 2. Applying and firing the counter enamel

See Chapter 5, steps 3 and 4.

When the Scalex is dry, turn the copper disc over, place it on a ceramic trivet (kept especially for this purpose) and carefully apply onto the bare (back) side an even coat of Klyr-Fire or similar binder that has been diluted 50% with distilled water. When applying the binder, make certain there are no air bubbles and that the binder covers the disc completely to the edges. If the binder "draws back," it is necessary to repeat Steps 1 and 2 before continuing with the remaining steps.

While the binder is still wet, sift an even coat of 80-mesh counter enamel onto the surface. Sufficient enamel should be applied so that the bare copper is no longer visible through the sifted enamel coating. Place the disc with the sifted enamel under the heat lamp and allow to dry.

When the counter enamel is completely dry, place the disc carefully on a stainless steel trivet assemblage and place into the kiln, protecting yourself with the recommended safety equipment. Fire the disc for approximately 2 minutes at 1500°F (816°C). After $1\frac{1}{2}$ minutes, check the firing process. When the enamel is fired to maturity, remove the assemblage from the kiln using the correct equipment and allow to cool in a draft-free environment away from other unfired enamels.

When the disc is cold to the touch, remove and discard the Scalex coating. Return your project to the pickle bath for approximately 5 minutes and proceed with the cleaning of the bare copper surface as described in Step 1. The working, or front, side of the disc is now ready for the application of the background enamel. The counter-enameled surface should be thoroughly neutralized after being exposed to the pickle bath.

Step 3. Applying and firing the background

To the clean copper surface, apply an even coat of diluted binder, checking for "draw back" characteristics. Sift onto the surface an even coat of 80-mesh enamel in your selected color. An opaque enamel in a light shade (white or pastel) is suggested. Observe all the application characteristics.

Allow the unfired enamel to dry under the heat lamp. Position the disc on a trivet assemblage and fire in the preheated kiln for approximately 2 minutes at 1500°F (816°C). Observing the courtesy rules, allow the piece to cool in a draft-free environment. It may be necessary to apply a second coat of your chosen background color. (If pits or holes occur, refer to the troubleshooting section in Chapter 12.)

When the desired background coating has been achieved, stone the edges of the disc, flush with running water, dry with a lint-free linen cloth, and proceed as follows.

Step 4. Transferring design onto enamel

Select a design to be transferred onto the enameled disc. Depending upon your creative ability, you may choose to work spontaneously upon the enamel surface, or to transfer design from your sketchbook. An 8008 Stabilo pencil or a water-soluble marker can be used directly on the enamel surface. Alternatively, a carbon paper which has no

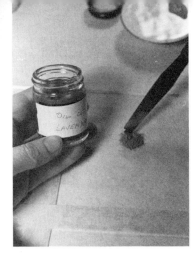

Fig. 8-7 *Place a small amount of painting enamel onto a sheet of glass.*

Fig. 8-8 *Mix with a selected oil.*

graphite or oil deposit can be successfully used to trace the design from your sketchbook onto the enamel surface. When fired, the transferred imagery, which is biodegradable, disappears and should not promote holes or pits.

Step 5. Mixing the painting enamel

Select the colors for your design. Opaques are recommended for this project. Prepare the painting enamels as described at the beginning of this project.

Onto a sheet of glass, place a small quantity of your chosen color, as shown in Figure 8-7, and carefully work into the powder a minute quantity of #5 thinning oil, oil of lavender, or oil of clove (Fig. 8-8). Allow the mixture to permeate, as the oil takes a short time to be absorbed into the powdered enamel. If a larger quantity of painting enamel is to be used, it can be mixed with the mixing medium in a small mortar and pestle.

For the painting technique, 350 to 400-mesh enamels can be mixed together to produce new shades and hues. This is the only time an optical mixing is not necessary, as the enamel particles are ground so finely that they appear to combine to make the new shade.

Alternatively, the painting enamel can be mixed with a little distilled water and water-soluble binder, such as Klyr-Fire (Figs. 8-9 and 8-10). Although this method does not produce the creamy consistency of the oil-based mixture, it does have its advantages. For enamelists who have enjoyed oil painting, application of the oil-based mixture gives great satisfaction (Fig. 8-11), whereas the painting enamels mixed with distilled water tend to work more like watercolors (Fig. 8-12).

  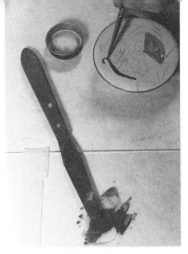

Fig. 8-9 *Mix with a little distilled water.*

Fig. 8-10 *Add two or three drops of binder, such as Klyr-Fire.*

Fig. 8-11 *Oil-painting effects can be obtained with oil-based painting enamel.*

Step 6. Limoges application

Using a variety of paintbrushes, apply the painting enamel mixture onto the enameled background. Apply as thinly as possible. When applied too thickly, the enamel surface will crack and craze during successive firings. To build up the color and opacity, it is advisable to apply several thin coats of the painting enamel, firing each coat after application.

All the colors planned for your design can be applied to the surface during one application. Or, continue with further applications of the painting enamel, building up form and colors until the design is complete. If you find that one color tends to bleed into its juxtaposed color, it is advisable to allow the existing one to dry before applying its neighboring color.

Allow the painting enamel to dry. When using an oil medium, the drying time will be greatly extended, even with the aid of a heat lamp. Since the oils are volatile, care should be taken that the enamel is thoroughly dry before putting it in the kiln. The painting enamel will look dull and flat when completely dry.

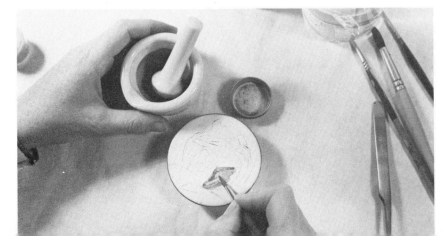

Fig. 8-12 *Painting enamel mixed with water and binder mixture can be applied like some watercolors.*

Step 7. Firing and finishing

Carefully place the dry enameled disc onto the kiln furniture assemblage and fire in the kiln, which has been preheated to 1450°F (787°C) for approximately $1\frac{1}{2}$ minutes. When painting grades of enamel are used, extra care must be taken not to overfire the piece. When painting enamel is fired at too high a temperature, or for too long a period of time, the image may spread and dissipate, especially with successsive firings

Allow the disc to cool and stone the edges.

Do not forget to keep an accurate record in your sketchbook: colors, firing times, number of applications, observations. These are all necessary gems of information that you will refer to time and again.

Fig. 9-1 Cacophony, 1981. Martha Banyas. Wallpiece, underglaze pencils and Limoges enamels on copper; $7\frac{1}{2}" \times 10" \times 1"$. Photograph, the artist.

·9·
Rendering with ceramic underglaze pencils

Rendering, or pencil drawing, is a rewarding technique for the artist who likes to sketch. A very different effect is created with this method of enameling. It can be used by itself, or incorporated with such other techniques as stencils or wet packing for equally pleasing results.

This project is a freer, more expressive approach to enameling than some of the more traditional techniques. It is offered here as the fifth project to help relieve some of the tension inexperienced enamelists sometimes undergo as they carefully and methodically follow instructions.

An inexpensive set of ceramic underglaze pencils is needed, usually available from ceramic suppliers or craft stores, and available in red,

Fig. 9-2 *Supplies for rendering project with underglaze pencils.*

blue, green, yellow, black, and brown. Sometimes other colors are available; if you enjoy this technique, it is advisable to seek out and acquire as many colors as possible. It must be remembered that ceramic underglaze pencils are not vitreous enamel. The composition is metallic oxides, which need to be absorbed into the enamel surface to become a permanent colorization of the enamel. When not fired into the glass body, the underglaze metallic oxides can be removed by washing and/or scrubbing.

Supplies

3-inch (76 mm) diameter, 18-gauge (1.024 mm)   Binder
   copper disc   Ceramic underglaze pencils
Enamels: Paintbrushes
   counter enamel, opaque white or pastel   Alundum stone
Scalex or similar

Step-by-step directions

Step 1. Preparing the metal disc

See Chapter 5, steps 1 and 2.

Clean a 3-inch (76 mm) 18-gauge copper disc by placing it in a pickle bath for approximately 5 minutes, or until it is a clean pink color. Remove the disc from the bath with copper tongs and wash off the pickle under running water.

Using your fingers as an applicator, apply powdered pumice to the surface of the metal. Scrub vigorously, working methodically over both front and back surfaces. When a bright, clean surface is achieved, give the copper disc a final wipe with saliva to neutralize the surface. Give the disc the water test for cleanliness.

Using a #12 brush, coat the front (image) side of the copper disc with a thick, even coat of liquid firescale inhibitor (Scalex or a similar product). Clean the brush under running water when the application is complete. Allow the Scalex-coated surface to dry. If a heat lamp is used, it will take 3 to 4 minutes; otherwise, let the Scalex air-dry until the surface is flat and dull.

Step 2. Applying and firing the counter enamel

See Chapter 5, steps 3 and 4.

When the Scalex is dry, turn the copper disc over, place it on a ceramic trivet and carefully apply onto the bare (back) side an even coat of binder that has been diluted 50% with distilled water. When applying the binder, make certain there are no air bubbles and that the binder covers the disc completely to the edges. If the binder "draws back," it is necessary to repeat step 1 before continuing with the remaining processes.

While the binder is still wet, sift an even coat of 80-mesh counter enamel onto the surface. Sufficient enamel should be applied so that the bare copper is no longer visible through the sifted enamel coating. Place the disc with the sifted enamel under the heat lamp and allow to dry.

When the counter enamel is completely dry, carefully place the disc on a stainless steel trivet assemblage. Place the assemblage into the kiln, protecting yourself with the recommended safety equipment. Fire the disc for approximately 2 minutes at 1500°F (816°C). After $1\frac{1}{2}$ minutes, check the firing process. When the enamel is fired to maturity, remove the assemblage from the kiln using the correct equipment and allow to cool in a draft-free environment away from other unfired enamels.

Step 3. Applying and firing background enamel

When the disc is cold to the touch, remove and discard the Scalex coating. Return your project to the pickle bath for approximately 5 minutes and proceed with the cleaning of the bare copper surface as described in Step 1. The counter-enameled surface should be thoroughly neutralized after being exposed to the pickle bath. The working, or front, side of the disc is now ready for the application of the background enamel.

To the clean copper surface, apply an even coat of diluted binder, checking for "draw back" characteristics. Sift onto the wet surface an even coat of 80-mesh enamel in your selected color. Again, it is suggested that you use an opaque enamel in a light shade (White T1000, TAW66 or similar). Observe all the application characteristics.

Allow the unfired enamel to dry under the heat lamp. Position the disc on a trivet assemblage and fire in the preheated kiln for approximately 2 minutes at 1500°F (816°C). Observing the courtesy rules, allow the piece to cool in a draft-free environment. It may be necessary to apply a second coat of your chosen background color. If pits or holes occur, refer to the troubleshooting section in Chapter 12.

When the desired background coating has been achieved, stone the edges of the disc, flush with running water, and proceed as follows.

Step 4. Achieving a matt surface

Before the ceramic underglaze pencils can be used, one more step must be carried out. The shiny enamel on the disc has to be stoned to a matt surface because the ceramic pencils will not mark on a regular shiny enamel surface.

Using the fine side of a flat Alundum stone, completely stone the entire working surface of the project under running water. It may be necessary to stop occasionally and dry the surface to check on your progress. The entire surface should have a flat, dull appearance when the stoning has been executed correctly. No shine should remain. Scrub off all stoning residue with a glass brush and flush well with running water. Dry thoroughly with a lint-free cloth. Care should be taken not to place fingers on the clean matt surface. If this does occur,

Fig. 9-3 *Stone the enamel surface flat with an Alundum stone.*

scrub again with the glass brush, flush well and dry. The matt finish will now take the underglaze ceramic pencils.

NOTE: There are four other methods of achieving a matt surface:

1. The surface can be sandblasted to a matt finish, if sandblasting equipment is available.

2. Acids may be used. Hydrofluoric acid treatment will produce the required flat surface, but it is highly dangerous and not recommended. Glaze etching solutions are also available, but again, their use is not recommended.

3. A commercial matt salt can be applied to the surface of the fired enamel. This salt will attack the shine and create a flat surface on which to work. This matt salt is imported from Europe and is available through Schauer Enamel Suppliers.

4. Use LF500 Matt White Enamel from Thompson's. This enamel will always remain matt, but it can be overcoated with a clear flux if a shiny finish is required. If a white finish is required, the LF500 Matt White Enamel should not be applied directly to bare copper: after firing, it will appear as a dull pink.

Step 5. Rendering with underglaze pencils

To execute a design onto the matt surface, proceed with normal rendering techniques. Cross-hatching and pencil strokes look good, characteristic of the drawing technique. Shading with a shading stick will enhance certain areas and provide contrasts.

As the color range available is generally limited to the six basic colors, shades and hues can be obtained by applying two or more colors together and blending with the shading stick. Or, two colors can be placed side-by-side, letting the eye mix them together; e.g., red and blue alternate to "produce" purple. Likewise, lighter shades can be produced by light pressure of a pencil onto the surface and darker shades by closer, heavier pressure of the pencils.

Experimentation is the key word, as many exciting variations can be produced. Upon application, the colors will appear light and pastel, but when fired, the darker and more intense colors will appear. This factor needs to be taken into consideration when designing the imagery.

Step 6. Firing

When you are satisfied with the imagery, blow away any excess pencil dust and fire the disc at 1450°F (788°C) for approximately 3 to 5 minutes. There is no waiting period for drying this time, as the pencils do not contain moisture and a binder was not used in their application. The firing time will vary considerably, as it depends on how thickly the pencil was applied. When the enamel is removed from the kiln, you

Fig. 9-4 *Rendering technique with ceramic under-glaze pencils.*

Fig. 9-5 *Light shades are produced by light pressure of the pencils, darker shades by denser, heavier pressure.*

will observe that the surface has regained its characteristic glossy appearance (unless LF500 Matt White was used).

Allow the enameled disc to cool. On inspection, after the enamel has cooled, there may still be a "bloom" or dusty appearance on the surface of the enamel. This is excess metallic oxide that has not been incorporated into the background surface. If it is too thick, it may never merge with the enamel, but a reasonable coating may be absorbed with additional firings. Do not touch the surface. Return the piece to the kiln for another 3 to 5 minutes at the 1450°F (788°C) temperature. Fire again, let cool and inspect. If the "bloom" is still apparent, refire once again, or allow to cool and remove the excess stains by brushing or washing away.

There is another alternative to this refiring technique: A coat of medium fusing flux (T1005 or LF303 for Matt White) can be fired over the pencil imagery, sealing in the ceramic underglaze. Utmost care must be taken during this firing process to ensure that the background enamel does not float and that the flux does not sink into the background. Too high a temperature or too long a firing time will promote this problem. The flux must also be perfectly clean.

Personal taste will play an important part in the decision to apply a flux overcoating. When flux is used, the pencil rendering has a definite appearance of being overglazed and trapped within. This, of course, is not necessarily detrimental.

Step 7. Subsequent renderings and firings

Additional pencil drawing may be added to the fired enamel. When the enamel is completely cool, the areas to be added to or modified should be stoned with an Alundum stone, as described in Step 4. The complete surface need not be stoned unless all the pencil work is to be retouched. Any area that is not to your liking can be completely erased by heavy stoning. Care should be taken not to stone completely through the background enamel to the bare copper. If this should occur, refer to the section on repairing enamels in Chapter 12.

Proceed with further pencil drawing and firing procedures as described in Steps 5 and 6, until you are satisfied with the results.

When totally satisfied with your pencil drawing project, stone the edges and finish as instructed in Chapter 11. Bring your sketchbook up-to-date.

For this project, the pencil drawing will look best on White (T1000 or TAW66), Ivory (T334) or Off White (T760) backgrounds. These surfaces are similar in color to normal sketchbook paper, which makes it easier to visualize the transfer of the imagery from paper to enamel. Also, the underglaze pencils tend to fire toward the pastel side. If the background color is too dark, the combined effect is sometimes lost.

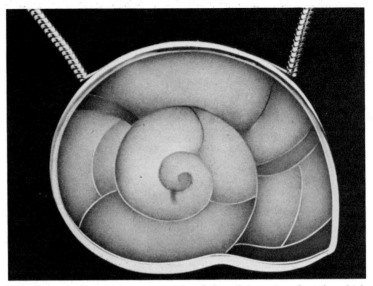

Fig. 10-1 Blue Shell #3, 1982. Carol Holaday. Cloisonné on fine silver, high satin finish; $1\frac{3}{8}"\ \times\ 1\frac{1}{8}"$. Photograph, the artist.

·10·
Cloisonné

The cloisonné technique has a long history, with outstanding examples from the Orient and Europe available for viewing in most art museums. Like many enameling terms, *cloisonné* is a derivative of a French word, *cloison,* meaning enclosed area or cell, which describes our sixth and final project.

Linear patterns of silver, gold or copper wire can be made by arranging the metal on its thin edge. These strips of metal become enclosed areas (or cells) to be filled with enamel. The expressive metal lines are a welcome addition to your enameling repertoire. In this project, transparent enamels can be used extensively for the first time.

Supplies

3-inch (76 mm) diameter, 18-gauge (1.024 mm)
    copper disc
Binder
Scalex or similar
Distilled water
Enamels:
    counter enamel, flux—hard fusing (T333),
        and selected transparent and opaque
        colors
Needlenose tweezers

Flat cloisonné wire:
    fine silver, 18 × 30 B & S gauge, (1.024 mm
        × 0.255 mm)
Plastic spoons or mixing tray
Inlay tools
Paintbrushes
Two eyedroppers
80-mesh sifter
Scissors or solder snips

Preparing the cloison wires

While working through the step-by-step procedures, there are many opportunities—while waiting for drying and/or cooling processes—to create your design and prepare the cloison wires for this project. However, since wire preparation is a fairly complex step in itself, this process will be covered before going on to the other procedures.

Although 24-karat yellow gold wire or copper wire can be used for cloisonné work, the cloisons for this project will be made from fine (pure) silver. The fine silver is soft, malleable and easily worked. The wire can be made from sheet, in the traditional manner, or bought ready for use from an enamel or jewelry supply house. It can be bought in a variety of thicknesses and depths, which should satisfy most artists' requirements. When the cloisonné wire is stiff and springy, it will require annealing before use (see page 38).

This cloisonné design should be simple without straight lines. A straight section of thin, flat wire is very difficult to stand on edge. Of course it can be done, but for this project, think of smooth-flowing curved lines. Remember that wires cannot be crossed physically: an optical crossing can be achieved with careful design construction. As you sketch, think of the pencil outline as the cloisonné wire line. The ideal shapes for the cloisons are compact, smooth, graceful curves. Practice with many sketches, drawing expressive minimal linear designs. Continuity will come with the placement of the enamels into the cells.

There are many ways to bend the wires to conform to the design in your sketchbook. One is to put a sheet of glass over the design and stick clear double-sided tape on the glass surface. The wires can now be bent and actually placed in position over the sketch (Fig. 10-4). The wires will hold their shape and remain in place while the remaining wires are worked on.

Another method is to bend the wires, working over the actual design, then transfer them to a tape arrangement on the lid of a container (Fig. 10-5). This method is excellent when a project is carried back and forth to the classroom: the cloisonné wires can be formed at the artist's

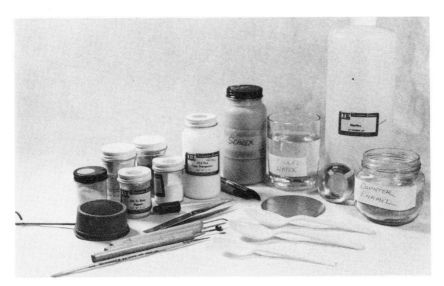

Fig. 10-2 Supplies for the cloisonné project.

convenience during relaxing periods at home. When carried inside the container, the wires cannot be squashed or damaged. The container can also be used to hold little scraps of wire and the cloisonné wire while it is in use.

Being soft and malleable, fine silver wire is easily formed with the fingers. Tiny jeweler's or watchmaker's needlenose pliers and tweezers are also useful (Fig. 10-6). If small circles are to be formed, the ends of paintbrushes can be used as mandrels (Fig. 10-7). Do not make the

Fig. 10-3 First Daisy. Bertie Wilson. Simple cloisonné design; opaque and transparent enamels on copper; 3" diameter.

Fig. 10-4 *Cloisonné wire can be positioned on double-sided tape attached to a sheet of glass, which is placed directly over the design.*

Fig. 10-5 *Or, the wires can be shaped over the actual drawing and transferred to tape, then attached to the lid of a container for portability.*

wires too long. Long, curved cells often cause the fired enamel to crack, as will two wires positioned close together (almost touching). Unnecessary kinks and bends can be removed by gently pulling the wire through your fingers several times.

As this is the first project for which transparent enamels will be used extensively, it is also necessary to prepare the transparent enamels, either by sifting or by washing, as described in Chapter 2. Enamel preparation, which remains the artist's choice, can also be done while preparing the disc for the cloisonné design.

Fig. 10-6 *Needlenose pliers are extremely useful for shaping cloisonné wire.*

Fig. 10-7 *The handle of an artist's brush is another helpful mandrel for bending cloisonné wire.*

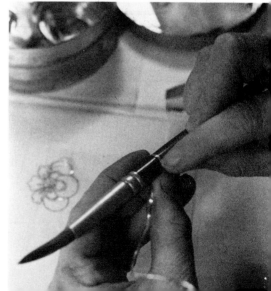

Step-by-step directions

Step 1. Preparing the copper disc

See Chapter 5, steps 1 and 2.

Clean a 3-inch (76 mm), 18-gauge (1.024 mm) copper disc by placing it in a pickle bath for approximately 5 minutes, or until it is a clean, pink color. Remove the disc from the bath with copper tongs and wash off the pickle under running water.

Using your fingers as an applicator, apply powdered pumice to the surface of the metal. Scrub vigorously, working methodically over both front and back surfaces. When a bright, clean surface is achieved, give the copper disc a final wipe with saliva to neutralize the surface. Give the disc the water test for cleanliness.

Coat the front (image) side of the copper disc with a thick, even coat of liquid firescale inhibitor (Scalex or a similar product), using a #12 brush. Clean the brush under running water when the application is complete. Allow the Scalex-coated surface to dry. If a heat lamp is used, it will take 3 to 4 minutes; otherwise, let the Scalex air dry until the surface is flat and dull.

Step 2. Applying and firing the counter enamel

See Chapter 5, steps 3 and 4.

When the Scalex is dry, turn the copper disc over, place it on a ceramic trivet (kept especially for this purpose) and carefully apply onto the bare (back) side an even coat of binder which has been diluted 50% with distilled water. When applying the binder, make certain there are no air bubbles and that the binder covers the disc completely to the edges. If the binder "draws back," it is necessary to repeat Step 1 before continuing with the remaining processes.

While the binder is still wet, sift an even coat of 80-mesh counter enamel onto the surface. Sufficient enamel should be applied so that the bare copper is no longer visible through the sifted enamel coating. Place the disc with the sifted enamel under the heat lamp and allow to dry.

When the counter enamel is completely dry, place the disc carefully on a stainless steel trivet assemblage. Place the assemblage into the kiln, protecting yourself with the recommended safety equipment. Fire the disc for approximately 2 minutes at 1500°F (816°C). After $1\frac{1}{2}$ minutes, check the firing process. When the enamel is fired to maturity, remove the assemblage from the kiln, using the correct equipment. Allow the project to cool in a draft-free environment away from other enamels.

Step 3. Applying and firing hard-fusing flux

When the disc is cold to the touch, remove and discard the Scalex coating. Return your project to the pickle bath for approximately 5 minutes and proceed with the cleaning of the bare copper surface as described in Step 1. Check the copper surface for any damage, scratches or marks: these imperfections must be removed completely, as they will show through the transparent enamels when the project is complete. Wet and dry paper, emery paper, or Bright Boy rubber abrasive wheels can be used to remove these marks. Alternatively, a texture incorporating these imperfections can be added to the background design.

The working, or front, side of the disc is now ready for the application of the flux. Flush well with running water and make sure the counter enamel has been neutralized. Dry with a lint-free linen cloth.

To the clean copper surface, apply an even coat of binder which has been diluted 50% with distilled water. Check for "draw back" characteristics. Sift onto the wet surface an even coat of Hard-Fusing Undercoat Flux (T333). This application of enamel should be kept as thin as possible. Observe all the application characteristics. You may note that the flux appears white at this stage (check the container, just in case you picked up white by mistake—it sometimes happens). The flux will fire to a transparent coating.

Allow the unfired enamel to dry under the heat lamp. Position the disc on a trivet assemblage and fire in a preheated kiln for approximately $1\frac{1}{2}$ to 2 minutes at 1600°F (871°C). Please note that this is a higher temperature than used previously for the opaque enamels.

Observing the courtesy rules, allow the piece to cool in a draft-free environment. If pits or holes occur, repair and refire as advised in Chapter 12. Two coats of flux should not be necessary.

When the desired background coating has been achieved, stone the edges of the disc, flush well with running water, dry with a lint-free linen cloth, and proceed as follows.

Step 4. Placing and firing the cloisons

Transfer your prepared cloisonné wire design to the enameled disc. Each section of wire should be carefully picked up from the adhesive tape with needlenose tweezers, dipped into the binder (which has been diluted 50% with distilled water and has been poured into a shallow dish) and positioned on the disc (Figs. 10-8 and 10-9). Do not flood the wires with binder (Fig. 10-10). The bottom edge of the wire is the only part that needs to be coated. When the binder is dry, it will hold the wire in position and keep the wires from slipping when the disc is placed in the kiln. If a wire has to be repositioned and the binder has already dried, add a drop of distilled water to the offending wire. The water will soften the binder so the wire can be easily removed. If you try to remove a wire that has been glued into position without softening the binder first, the wire will be pulled out of shape. When all the wires are in position, leave the disc to dry. Each wire should be standing straight up on its thin edge, perpendicular to the base.

Fig. 10-8 *Coat the bottom edge of each cloison with diluted binder.*

Fig. 10-9 *Position each coated cloison on the previously enameled disc.*

Fig. 10-10 *Do not flood the cloisons with the binder, as was done here.*

It is not advisable to carry the disc around until the binder has dried. On this occasion do not try to move the disc to the heat lamp; leave it where you have been working. The wire has a tendency to slip from the enameled surface while the binder is wet, especially on concave and convex surfaces. Drying should only take a few minutes as there are no enamel granules.

When the binder is dry, carefully move the disc to a trivet assemblage; one slight jolt will send the wires scattering. Firing times are now most critical. The fine silver cloisonné wire has a melting temperature of 1761°F (960°C). This may seem far beyond the temperatures used, but if the disc is left in the kiln too long, even at a lower temperature, the internal heat of the disc can build up and within a few seconds, the cloisonné wires will start to melt. This phenomenon is known as a eutectic action: the melting-flowing point of two elements (copper and silver, in this case) is at a temperature substantially lower than that of either metal if heated separately.

There is also the possibility that if the background flux becomes too liquid, the cloisonné wires will sink into the enamel. Nothing can be done to recover the wires in either circumstance.

Fire the disc and cloisonné wires for approximately $1\frac{1}{2}$ minutes at 1500°F (816°C). An indication that the wires have bonded to the background flux is when a thin, glossy line appears at the base of each wire (Fig. 10-11); a visual check is better than a timed firing. At this point, remove the assemblage from the kiln and place it on a heat-resistant surface. Immediately, while the enamel flux is still liquid, carefully touch the tops of the cloisonné wires with a scrolling tool or spatula, to assure a good bond between the enamel and the wire (Fig. 10-12). Do *not* press hard, or the wires may collapse. Remove to the draft-free cooling area and allow to cool.

Step 5. Mixing and inlaying enamels

When the disc has cooled, check the wires to make sure they are all securely afixed to the enamel. Carefully stone the edges of the disc under running water, pat dry with a lint-free linen cloth, and return the disc to your worktable.

If some of the wires are not bonded onto the surface, return the disc to the kiln and repeat the firing process. If loose wire is only a minor problem, it is not necessary to refire until the enamels have been added.

Use a plastic spoon or a watercolor tray as a mixing bowl for each color (Fig. 10-13). With a water-soluble marker, record the enamel color and number on each handle or compartment. Mix each color of your prepared transparent enamels with one or two drops of binder and enough distilled water to make a thin paste. Mix carefully, trying not to create bubbles. Allow the mixtures to settle for a few minutes.

Scoop up a small quantity of the enamel mixture with the wet inlay spatula; then, with the wet inlay applicator, carefully fill the cloisons with the selected colors (Fig. 10-14). The enamel mixture should be a little more moist than the wet packing mixture for project 2 (Ch. 6). For very small areas, apply the enamel with a fine sable-hair paintbrush (#000). When using a paintbrush, use a dabbing technique rather than trying to apply the enamel like oil paint. Work carefully, taking care not to cover the cloison wires. Any enamel that dries on the top of the wires can be removed with a #000 paintbrush dampened with a little water. Pack into the cloison cells a good even coat of enamel not more than three grains high. Excess water in the cloisons should be blotted up with a Q-Tip or the edge of a paper towel. It is better to fire the piece several times than to try to fill the cloisons completely in one firing. Several thin coats will also give greater transparency.

Colors can be blended together within the cloison areas to produce

Fig. 10-11 *When the piece is fired correctly, a thin glossy line will be visible at the base of each cloison.*

Fig. 10-12 *While the enamel is still liquid, gently touch the cloison wires with the edge of a tool, to assure a good bond between the enamel and the cloisons.* Do not press hard.

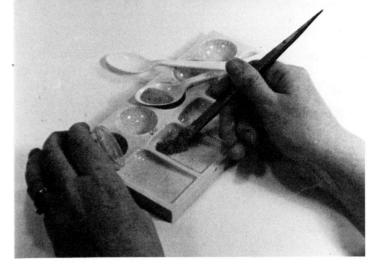

Fig. 10-13 Mix the prepared enamels in a watercolor tray, or in plastic spoons.

shading. Opaque enamels can be introduced to provide varying degrees of depth and contrast. An enamel which has only transparents can often appear uninteresting, whereas subtle combinations of transparent and opaque enamels can add diversity and excitement.

Often, opaques can be applied as the first coat, with subsequent coats of transparent. This technique may produce an opal-like quality or the translucence of alabaster. When applying transparents over dark opaques, use a transparent of the same shade or several shades lighter. With light opaques, use a flux. Clear flux over a dark opaque may appear milky when the fines have not been removed.

Step 6. Firing the cloisonné enamel

Leave the applied enamels to dry thoroughly. Again check the top edges of the cloisons for unwanted grains of enamel. Position the disc

Fig. 10-14 Using a wet inlay spatula and inlay applicator, fill the cloisons with selected colors.

Fig. 10-15 Use an artist's brush to apply enamel to small cloisons.

Fig. 10-16 Pack each cell evenly, not more than three enamel grains high. Tap side of disk to even out coating.

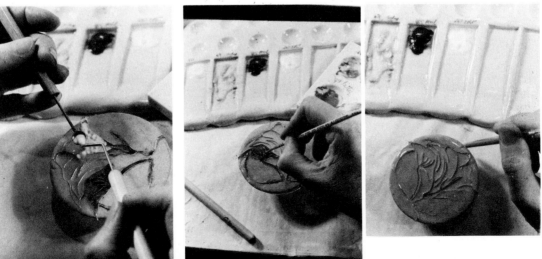

on a trivet assemblage and place in the preheated kiln. Fire at 1500°F (816°C) for approximately 1½ minutes. Watch the firing temperatures and time closely. Again, it is most critical to keep the cloisonné wires from melting. Remove the enamel assemblage from the kiln and allow to cool on a heat-resistant surface in a draft-free environment.

You will now observe that the fired enamel in each cloison is concave; if you like this effect and are happy with the colors, you may declare your project complete, and proceed with the usual finishing procedures.

However, we will follow through the processes, producing an enamel where the cloisonné wires and the enamel all share the same common level and the surface is finished in a matt or glossy polish.

Step 7. Subsequent enamel inlay

Stone the edges of the disc carefully. Any enamel that has been fired onto the wires can be delicately stoned to remove it. Do *not* press hard with the stone; the wires can still collapse. When stoning an enamel surface, it is an excellent idea to place the enameled disc on a wooden board. This board will protect the disc from flexing; an enamel that is bent or flexed will crack very easily. Glass-brush under running water, flush well, and dry with a lint-free cloth.

Return the disc to your work area and apply another layer of the prepared enamels (Fig. 10-17). If the enamels in the mixing containers have dried, add two to three drops of distilled water. When all the colors have been applied, let the disc dry. Fire at 1500°F (816°C) for approximately 1½ minutes. Again, allow to cool, then stone edges and wires where necessary. Apply further coats of enamel and fire after each application until the fired enamel is flush with (or a fraction above) the cloisons.

Fig. 10-17 *Apply further layers of the prepared enamels until the desired results are achieved.*

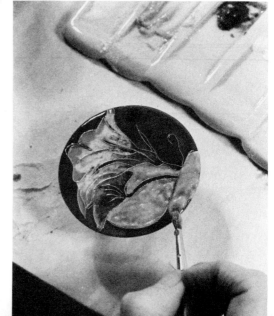

Finishing alternatives

Several decisions can be made as to the aesthetic finish for your cloisonné enamel. You may choose to leave the surface just as it comes out of the kiln on its last firing. Or, if you want to have the smooth, flat cloisonné look that most people are familiar with, the entire working surface has to be stoned, then finished to a matt surface, a semi-gloss finish, or a highly polished surface. For complete explanation of these finishing techniques, see Chapter 11. Whatever finish you decide upon for this cloisonné project is your own personal preference: exciting qualities can be found in each type of finish. No way is more correct than another—it is all a point of view.

Finish off your sketchbook notes and observations. From this point on, your skills should develop in leaps and bounds; explore; experiment; become a creative enamel artist.

PART • THREE

For your information

Overleaf: Memory of a Childhood Toy. *Diana Whitmer-Francko. Cloisonné enamel with foils; silver, bronze, copper; $2\frac{1}{4}'' \times 2\frac{7}{8}'' \times 2\frac{1}{2}''$. Photograph, the artist.*

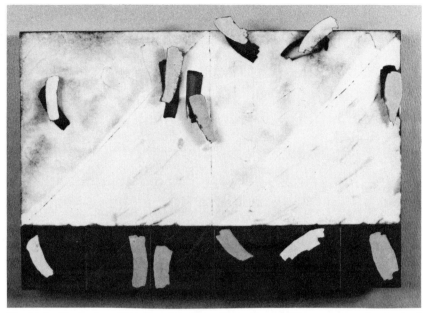

Fig. 11-1 Six Strokes, 1981. Gretchen Goss. Champlévé and Limoges pierced and raised shapes; 8″ × 12″. Photograph, The Cleveland Museum of Art.

·11·
More on enameling

Alternative enamel application

There are two methods of application for sifting enamel onto a metal surface: *wet* and *dry*. If you are a beginning enamelist, follow the recommendations for applying enamels in the six projects in Part Two before trying alternate methods. (Oftimes an inexperienced enamelist will have difficulty getting a project into the kiln without losing enamel along the way.) With a little experience and confidence, the choice of wet or dry application will become the individual's personal preference.

Enamel that has been graded by sifting or enamel that has been washed is particularly difficult to apply dry. The variations in particle

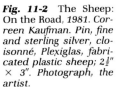

Fig. 11-2 The Sheep: On the Road, *1981. Correen Kaufman. Pin, fine and sterling silver, cloisonné, Plexiglas, fabricated plastic sheep; 2½" × 3". Photograph, the artist.*

size are actually an aid to dry application; each granule bonds with the next to become a cohesive network, creating a natural tension. This tension will hold the dry enamel in place, even on a slightly curved surface. Lead-free enamels are particularly good for dry sifting.

The advantage to dry sifting is that there is no organic holding agent, such as Klyr-Fire, to interfere with the enamel maturing during firing. Organic holding agents or binders have to be burnt away during the firing process. The binders turn to gases, which must escape from the maturing enamel surface, and appear as bubbles. These bubbles are

Fig. 11-3 Various types and sizes of sifters. Courtesy of Seaire Manufacturing.

only observed in transparent enamels, where they may produce a lack of transparency and are often confused with "dirty enamels." They can also be present in opaques, but are not noticeable.

Binders are quite necessary when steep-sided vessels are to be enameled with granular enamel, or under other circumstances where the enamel must be held in place before firing. The choice remains one for the individual, who must decide whether transparency or holding power is more critical for a specific piece.

When applying transparents by the wet packing or painting methods, the choice again must be made whether a binder should be added to the wet enamels. It is a matter of manipulation: if the enamel will stay in place without a binder, do not add it. An enamel without additives should fire to a greater transparency, with no apparent gas bubbles. Thin applications of enamel also aid greater transparency.

Fig. 11-4 Multicolor surface sample panel.

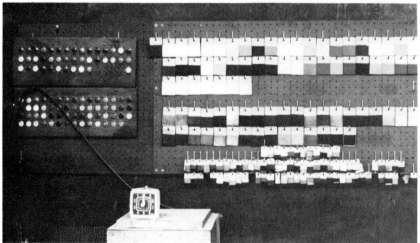

Fig. 11-5 Sample panels with one color each. Courtesy of Ceramic Coating Company.

Fig. 11-6 *Color sample disc attached to lid of enamel container; note the surface textures.*

Fig. 11-7 *Manufacturer's color sample attached to enamel container, with multisurface sample on lid.*

Color sample test panels

Making color sample test panels can be laborious and time consuming. However, a serious enamelist should have a ready-reference to how each color reacts and appears on various surfaces. Prior to important projects, it is advisable to run retests of the colors chosen on the same metal to be used for the project. Slightly different firing temperatures and base metals may produce a variance in color. The juxtaposition of color may also produce a different optical effect, so it is good to check color compatibility.

How the test panels are made is purely the preference of the enamelist. Some prefer to have all the colors and varying surfaces on a single panel (Fig. 11-4), while others prefer individual panels for each color (Fig. 11-5). The advantage of the latter is that you can arrange and rearrange the panels to work out your color schemes.

One excellent arrangement is to have a small sample disc glued to the top of each enamel container. Glue the printed color sample from the manufacturer's color guide to the front of the container as well, for a quick comparison to your fired sample.

Whatever method you choose for making your color samples, the tests should include:

1. Transparents over bare copper with a smooth metal surface
2. Transparents over bare copper with a textured metal surface
3. Transparents over flux, smooth metal surface
4. Transparents over flux, textured metal surface
5. Transparents over white opaque enamel
6. Transparents over gold foil
7. Transparents over silver foil

Test panels for opaques and opalescents are much easier, as the base metal or color does not necessarily affect their appearance. Be aware, though, that the base metal can sometimes affect the color of the enamel, depending upon the chemical makeup of the enamel; metal opacity, and thickness also contribute to color variances.

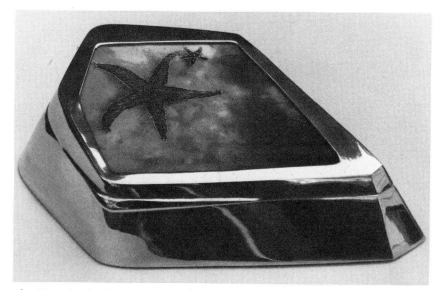

Fig. 12-1 Starfish box. Joanne Stasik-Conant. Silver cloisonné on copper with gold foil and silver beads; pewter container; 4" × 5" × 3". Courtesy of the Spring Street Enamels Gallery.

·12·
Refining, finishing and mounting enamels

The final firing has taken place, and, after all the long hours and diligent labor, your enamel now requires its finishing touches. Without careful refining, all those long hours of loving work will not show. A little extra care now makes all the difference in producing a really creative enamel you will be proud to say you made.

Depending upon the scale in which you work, the enamel may become a piece of jewelry, a wall hanging, or a platter for the coffee table. With any project, the edges need final attention before mounting, setting or displaying.

Fig. 12-2 *Files and wet-and-dry paper for finishing edges.*

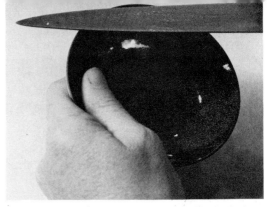

Fig. 12-3 *Use the rounded side of the file to take long, sweeping strokes.*

Refining the edges

Using a #2 half-round file, file both the front and back edges of the enamel. File at an oblique angle to the surface, using the rounded side of the file (Fig. 12-3). Make long, sweeping strokes. The enamel is cut first, followed by the metal. Work methodically around all edges. When complete, perform this process again with a #4 half-round file, using the same technique. File both the front and the back of the project in this manner. The center of the metal becomes the point of contact for frames or bezels or for support with your fingers. This same process can be achieved by grinding with an Alundum stone under running water. The choice is yours.

Wash off all residue and, working under running water, use a small piece of #320 wet-and-dry paper to carefully finish off the filed edge. Care should be taken not to abrade the enamel surfaces.

When the refinement of the edges is complete, the surface of the enamel needs a good wash with pure liquid soap and warm water. Dry with a lint-free linen cloth. Your hands should not touch the enamel surfaces. Any time you wish to pick up the enamel, handle only the exposed copper edges. Body oils and acids can contaminate the enamel surfaces and cause deterioration in years to come. Unless you will be using one of the special cloisonné finishes discussed below, the enamel is now ready for mounting.

Cloisonné finishes

Personal preference should guide your aesthetic decision as to what style and type of final finish to use on a cloisonné enamel, which may be concave, convex or flat.

1. *Concave.* Each cell in a concave cloisonné has less enamel in its center than around the cloisonné wires, giving it a concave appearance. Capillary attraction during firing achieves this effect. Apply several thin coats of enamel and fire in between.

To finish, carefully stone the cloisonné wires with an Alundum stone to remove excess enamel. Extra care needs to be taken so that the wires do not bend with the pressure of the stone. The wires can also delaminate from the enamel when too much friction is produced during the stoning process. Glass-brush thoroughly to remove all stoning residue.

2. *Convex*. Convex cloisonné is the exact opposite of concave cloisonné. The enamel is fired to a rounded, sculptural convex surface slightly above each cloisonné wire. Great care has to be exercised with firing times and temperatures. Just a moment too long, or too hot a temperature, will send the enamel cascading over the wires, burying the cloisonné design forever.

Throughout the firing processes, the cloisons must be kept absolutely clean of all enamel granules. Because of the cushion-like surface, it is extremely difficult to clean the wires after the final firing.

3. *Flat*. Flat cloisonné is the most common type. The wires and the enamel surface both share the same flat plane. This type of cloisonné can be given a matt, semi-gloss, or high-gloss finish.

Fig. 12-5 Sweet Pea, 1982. Glenice Lesley Matthews. Pin, transparent and opalescent convex cloisonné enamel on fine silver; set in sterling silver with moonstone; 1¾″ diameter.

Fig. 12-4 Humming Bird *container, 1981. Mary Koch. Transparent concave enamel on fine silver, sterling silver container; 2½″ diameter, 3″ high.*

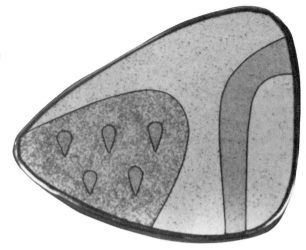

Fig. 12-6 *Pin, 1982. Alison Howard Levy. Opaque cloisonné on fine silver, with mixing of opaque colors to achieve stonelike effect; sterling silver setting; roller texture on back; stoned to a matt finish with a Scotch stone; $1\frac{3}{4}'' \times 1\frac{1}{4}'' \times \frac{1}{4}''$. Photograph, the artist.*

Matt finish

Matt finishes are often seen on enamels from the German schools. This surface gives very satisfying results, but requires time and "elbow grease."

After several applications of enamel and firings, the enamel and the cloisonné wires should all be at a similar level (Fig. 12-7). Under running water, carefully stone the complete surface, working over both the

Fig. 12-7 *After several applications of enamel, the wire and the enamel should be level.*

Fig. 12-8 *After stoning, some voids may still be visible.*

Fig. 12-9 *Flash fire after stoning to achieve a smooth gloss finish, with wires and enamel at one level.*

wires and the enamel. Use an Alundum stone and support the enamel on a board. The support of the board eliminates the risk of flexing the enamel, which would cause it to crack. The piece may need to be dried once or twice to check your progress. When the surface is continuous, without bumps or voids, glass brush thoroughly, again working under running water. Check the surface again.

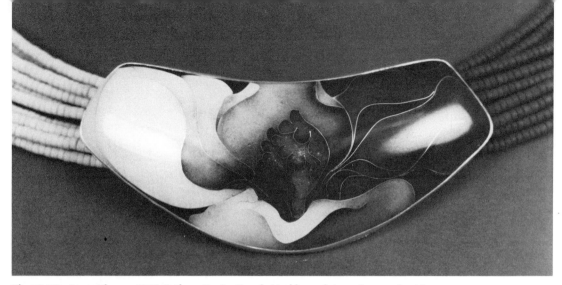

Fig. 12-10 Inner Flower, 1980. Kathryn Regier Gough. Necklace, cloisonné enamels with wet-and-dry paper finish; porcelain beads; $3\frac{1}{4}" \times 1\frac{3}{4}"$. Photograph, the artist.

If there are very deep voids, it is advisable to stop the stoning, refill the voids with enamel, and refire (Figs. 12-8 and 12-9). Otherwise, you may stone away half the thickness of the cloisonné piece before a common level is found. After firing and cooling, stone the surface again as described above.

When an even, flat surface has been achieved, change the stone for 325 wet-and-dry paper. Again working under running water, paper the cloisonné until all stoning marks are removed and the surface feels as smooth as silk. Glass brush thoroughly and dry.

Fig. 12-11 Cloisonné box. Ellen Kaufman. Box lid is a pendant; silver cloisonné and foils, transparent enamels, gloss finish; $2\frac{1}{4}" \times 3\frac{1}{2}"$. Photograph, Jay Kaufman.

Finally, apply paste wax to the entire surface and, after drying, buff with a soft cloth. Two coats of wax are recommended.

Semigloss finish

On completion of the stoning, and any refiring that may be necessary, a very pleasing semigloss finish can be produced on the cloisonné surface by using lapidary techniques. This type of finish is best carried out on special lapidary equipment, but it can also be successfully completed by hand with a little extra time and special effort.

Using the various grades of grinding and polishing compounds, a cloisonné enamel can be shaped and polished using the same procedures used to polish semiprecious cabochon stones. The final result is a smooth, slick semigloss finish which is very pleasing to feel. Using this same technique, a full gloss finish can be achieved by continuing with fine grades of the grinding and polishing compounds on the lapidary wheel. A final buffing with Tripoli followed by rouge will give the cloisonné a professional glow.

High-gloss finish

A high-gloss finish is achieved by a final "flash firing" after all stoning and refilling of voids has been completed. Great care is needed with this final firing, as a moment too long in the kiln may be disastrous.

Thoroughly glass brush the entire surface of the enamel before firing. Any residue from stoning or wet-and-dry paper that is left on the surface will fire into the enamel, imparting a grey scum that cannot be removed.

Flash fire the carefully prepared cloisonné enamel for a scant 75 seconds at 1450°F (788°C). The surface will be restored to the familiar surface of a glossy enamel.

Enamels for jewelry

Many good books are available to instruct you on jewelry-making techniques. Treat your enamel like a fragile cabochon stone and set according to the manual's instructions. Many creative and innovative designs that incorporate the enamel and the metal setting will produce exciting results. Be sensitive to the media and choose settings that blend, rather than contrast. Settings that protect the enamel are also advisable, e.g., a claw setting is not protective, whereas a bezel setting helps to protect the edges of the enamel against chipping.

Use either high-karat gold or fine silver for the bezels. Other grades of metals are too resistant and, when pressure is applied to the metal while setting the enamel, it can cause the enamel to crack under the stress.

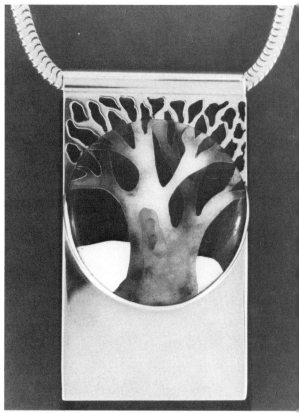

Fig. 12-12 *Pendant. Ellen Kaufman. Gold cloisonné, foils, transparent enamels, 14K gold setting, mabé pearl and ruby. Photograph, Jay Kaufman.*

Fig. 12-13 White Tree, 1979. *Kathryn Regier Gough. Necklace, cloisonné enamel; cut and pierced sterling silver setting pegged to ebony; $2\frac{5}{8}'' \times 1\frac{5}{8}'' \times \frac{1}{2}''$. Photograph, the artist.*

Fig. 12-14 Foil Series. Thomas S. Farrell. Transparent and opaque enamels and foil on copper; set in fine silver and sterling silver; 14K gold, jade; 1″ × 1½″ × ¼″. Photograph, Barbara Mail.

Fig. 12-15 Belt buckle. Linda Sherman. Silver cloisonné, transparent enamels, sterling silver setting; 3″ × 2½″. Courtesy of the Spring Street Enamels Gallery.

Never, *never* drill or punch a hole in your project and thread it on a chain or cord. This will give the enamel, which has taken you so long to produce, the appearance of an inferior—dime-store—product. It deserves the added time and effort to make it into a beautiful piece of jewelry.

Enamels for containers

Small enamels can be used most successfully as lids for wood, metal or ceramic containers. It is easy to glue an enamel onto a surface with no sensitivity to the relationship between media.

Fig. 12-16 Container. Belle and Roger Kuhn. Transparent enamels on fine silver; textured foil, sterling silver; 1″ × 2″ × 3″. Photograph, the artists.

Fig. 12-17 Stonehenge Revisited. *Shirley Rosenthal. High-fired opaque enamels on copper, mounted on Plexiglas; 24" × 36". Photograph, the artist.*

Fig. 12-18 Jigsaw, 1982. *Rebecca Brannon. Enamel on copper and wood; 18" × 12". Photograph, the artist.*

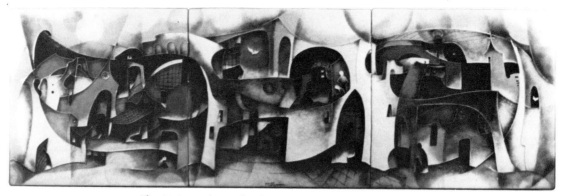

Fig. 12-19 Urban Life: The Uprooted. *Marian Slepian. Fine silver cloisonné on copper; three 12" panels, relief mounted on Lucite; 19" × 43". Photograph, the artist.*

Fig. 12-20 Sounding. *Duncan Berry. Miniature table screen; three panels in cloisonné and 23K gold; opaques and transparents over copper; deep relief carved walnut frame by Rene Soulard; 14" × 24". Photograph, the artist.*

When a ceramic or wooden box is used as the recipient of the enamel, a complete and finished look can be obtained by adding some type of framework to the enamel. It may be just a simple wire around the edge of the enamel or, if you have silversmithing skills, a pure silver bezel. Not only does the enamel gain prestige by this addition, it also gives the enamel extra protection. The finished result is worth the extra effort and the professional appearance will be most satisfying.

Gold, silver, pewter, brass, copper, or other metal containers require special silversmithing skills. There are many technical manuals available (see Further Reading list). Nothing is quite so satisfying as constructing a special metal container on which to mount your enamel.

Wall hangings and plaques

An enamel that hangs on a wall needs the same sensitive approach to its mounting as an enamel that is used in jewelry or containers. So often, a well-thought-out and beautifully executed enamel is simply glued on a piece of mattboard and hurriedly framed for display. It will always remain just that: an enamel stuck on a piece of board and framed. No correlation between one surface and the other will exist. Have pride in your work and follow through from the original concept to its final conclusion.

Many materials may be used to mount the enamels: Plexiglass, wood, metal, cloth, mattboard; even a pre-enameled steel title can be used effectively. An enamel plaque can be mounted to give a free-floating appearance, or set into the mounting, or matt, similar to framing a picture. Sometimes the addition of a bezel again helps strengthen the composition before it is mounted onto another material.

Think the complete project through, imagine it as it hangs on the wall. The enamel is not completed until it is presented in its final form.

Fig. 13-1 Handpiece in two parts, Aperture Series. Colette. Brooch and neckpiece enclosed in sculpture; 24K gold cloisonné on fine silver, set in 24K gold; electroformed bronze, anodized aluminum; 6" × 8" × 5". Photograph, the artist.

·13·
Troubleshooting or "don't give up — there's always hope"

When an artist comes anew to enameling, with anticipation running high, sometimes an enamel is removed from the kiln with pit holes, crazing or other undesirable defects. Do not worry, and do not be disappointed; this happens to everyone. Even the most experienced enamelist can encounter these problems.

If you understand what has happened, it is often easy to correct an enamel; even when all else fails, *do not throw it out*. Many creative and exciting enamel pieces have been produced by "mistakes." The best advice is to keep an open mind and be flexible until the project is declared finished.

A number of common problems and possible solutions are discussed in this chapter. Remember, though, that only the person working on the enamel can ascertain through experience what really caused a defect; and, if one suggested solution does not work, adopt another. Keep an open mind and persevere.

Bare metal patches (pebble effect)

DEFECT: Bare patches, or pebbling, are often caused by an insufficient layer of enamel on the bare metal (Fig. 13-2). When the enamel in the kiln changes from its dry particle state to its liquid form, the volumes change and each enamel particle draws up. This leaves the surface with areas of enamel and areas of bare metal. When the piece is removed from the kiln, you will have a salt-and-pepper effect of bare metal areas and enameled areas or spots. Each enameled spot will resemble a small conical mound.

SOLUTION: Use the correct amount of enamel. To repair this fault, cool, pickle, wash thoroughly, glass brush and neutralize the piece. If the piece is flat, apply another coat of enamel without a binder and refire. If your project is shaped, a binder may be needed; but note that this defect can be aggravated by the use of excessive binder with insufficient enamel. The gas from the organic matter (binder) also helps to separate the enamel.

Fig. 13-2 *Bare metal patches, or pebble effect, caused by insufficient enamel.*

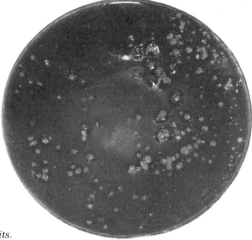

Fig. 13-3 *Craters, bubbles and pits.*

Craterous bubbles and pits

DEFECT: If your enamel comes out of the kiln with craterous bubbles and pits (Fig. 13-3), it is often the sign of insufficient preparation, contamination of the surface of the metal, or contamination of the enamel. Pickle, pumice or oil remnants are often the cause of this problem. These problems are usually encountered with the first coat on bare metal.

SOLUTION: Always pay strict attention to the cleanliness of the metal. Cool and pickle the piece until clean. Flush thoroughly with running water and neutralize. It is most important that no residues remain down inside those craters (a WaterPik is an excellent flushing tool). Unlike the characteristics of the pebbling defect, where the enamel is sealed to the copper in little mounds, the problem with craters or pits is that the exposed copper surface is greater than the top opening (just like a volcano). These craters will retain contaminants if not prepared with attentive care. Any bubbles present in the surface also need attention. They should be broken with a sharp tool (protect your eyes from the possibility of flying glass). It is advisable to do this after the piece has been pickled and washed. When you are satisfied that all the craters are free of contaminants and all the bubbles have been opened, carefully place dry enamel into the craters, mounding the enamel slightly above each rim. Do not use a binder, as it will produce a difference in color. (This is caused by the fines present in unwashed enamels; as the binder dries, it draws the fines toward the edge of each pit hole. Upon firing, the fines will be visible as a difference in color.) Refire at the required temperature and allow to cool. Sometimes it is necessary to apply another coat of the same color before proceeding.

Burnout

DEFECT: Upon taking the enamel project from the kiln, you notice the enamel has drawn up into thick rivulets, exposing the copper in some places (Fig. 13-4). Enamel may have also moved away from the edges. These are the effects of over-firing and the uneven application of enamel. Transparents often take on a bright greenish appearance, a result of copper oxides combining with the enamel to produce their own coloration. Some opaques will change color and may even become transparent. The lighter opaque shades can also have green edges.

SOLUTION: When cool, pickle until clean, wash thoroughly, and neutralize. The thick enamel areas can be stoned down to an acceptable thickness, then another coat of enamel applied to the complete surface and refired.

Sometimes, the burnout effect is artistically pleasing and the coloration desirable. In this case, you may choose to make the "accident" pay off. Wipe away loose firescale (greenish-black flakes) from the bare

Fig. 13-4 *Burnout, due to overfiring or uneven enamel application.*

Fig. 13-5 *Firescale contamination shows up as unsightly black spots.*

metal areas, stone where the enamel is too thick, and apply a coat of medium fusing flux and refire. Alternatively, wet pack the exposed metal areas with a contrasting color. This spontaneous "accident" may be a future masterpiece!

Firescale (greenish-black flecks)

DEFECT: On the surface of the fired enamel is a variety of dull black spots which are aesthetically disastrous (Fig. 13-5). These flecks are

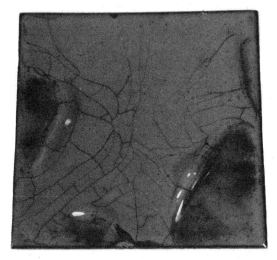

Fig. 13-6 *Peeling enamel, caused by overfiring, contamination, or wet firing.*

probably firescale—small particles of oxides from bare copper or scale from the stainless steel trivets. The firescale could have contaminated your enamel either prior to firing or during the firing process in the kiln. Copper scale will create a black speck which turns brick red or green on successive firings and diffuses into the enamel. Stainless steel scale will create a black speck which will stay black. This scale has straight edges and will always retain that form. Scale from kiln furniture frequently has enamel on it also.

When a piece of bare, hot copper is cooling, the black firescale will pop off the surface and become airborne. This firescale is a potential contaminant to open bottles of enamel in your work area or may deposit itself upon an enamel surface that is waiting to be fired. The best remedy for this problem is to always segregate unfired and fired surfaces and keep your enamel containers covered.

Firescale in the kiln is not so easy to deal with, although there are several precautions you can take:

1. Use another kiln or a silversmithing torch for annealing.

2. Cover bare copper surfaces with Scalex or a similar scale retardant before the metal is placed in the kiln.

3. Clean the kiln and use kiln wash on a regular basis.

4. Keep all kiln furniture clean and free of flaking particles.

Black specks can also be copper filings from the edges of the projects on which you have been working. If you use the filing method for maintenance and refinement of enamel edges, do your filing in an area well away from your and others' enameling and firing workspace. SOLUTION: Remove the firescale from the fired enamel by either grinding away the offending spots with a heatless grinder wheel on a flex-shaft, or by stoning the areas with an Alundum stone. Whatever method is used, be sure to flush the surface thoroughly with water after the removal process is complete. Use a glass brush to give the surface that final, thorough scrubbing. Residues from the grinding wheel and/or stone, if allowed to remain, can cause future pits or irregular surfaces with further firings.

If the contaminating specks are deep, or are on a cloisonné enamel, a diamond drill can be used to drill away the offending speck. Again clean the surface thoroughly after the contaminants have been removed. Flush drilled holes thoroughly; you do not want to replace one foreign body with another.

Peeling enamel

DEFECT: There are three types of peeling that can cause problems for the enamelist:

1. Enamel that peels or flakes off while the fired piece is cooling.

2. Enamel that crawls or peels away from the metal surface may have been applied too thickly over firescale or onto a contaminated surface.

3. Enamel that pulls back may have been damp when fired.

The first problem (1) can be caused by firing the piece too long or at too low a temperature. The copper forms firescale under the enamel before the enamel granules are softened and have had time to flow together to form a closed surface. The enamel then adheres to the scale, but the scale is not attached to the copper. Upon cooling, the scale pulls away from the copper due to the differing contraction rates. The flakes of enamel will have a brick-red interface (backside).

The second problem (2) occurs when using firescale deposits on copper for decorative effects. if the metal surface has been highly oxidized (black copper oxide) before the enamel application, during the firing process the enamel may crawl or peel away from the metal surface. This is caused by the firescale deposit being too thick. The peeling and the pulling back are two different occurrences. Unclean surfaces, such as those with heavy oil deposits, can also cause the enamel to either peel back due to excessive oxides, or pull back due to non-wetting of the surface by the enamel.

The last problem (3) is caused by placing the project into the kiln while the applied binder/water/enamel surface is still damp. If you are observant, this can be detected as steam rising from the surface. If left in situ, the enamel as it matures will pull back from the metal or previously enameled surfaces.

SOLUTION: As with all other problems mentioned, it is advisable to clean the problem areas, patch and refire. When firescale on the metal surface is to be used as part of the design, it is advisable to keep it to a minimum thickness, which will allow the enamel to penetrate the firescale and bond to the solid metal during firing.

Cracks

DEFECT: Cracks that appear during the working stages should be considered and handled differently than those which appear through misuse or abuse of a finished enamel.

Circular, haphazard or straight cracks in first enamel coat

Cracks that appear in the first coat of enamel usually fall into three categories.

1. Circular Cracks (Fig. 13-7). These occur when the enamel surface is uneven and too heavy. This is especially true when enameling on thin metal that has not been counter-enameled.

2. Haphazard Cracks (Fig. 13-8). Cracks that change direction in paths occur when the piece has been cooled too rapidly, or touched at the wrong time with a cold tool.

Fig. 13-7 *Circular cracks, usually the result of uneven, heavy enamel.*

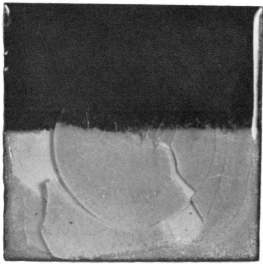

Fig. 13-8 *Haphazard cracks, usually the result of cooling an enamel too rapidly.*

3. Straight Cracks (Fig. 13-9). The occurrence of straight cracks is caused by uneven tension on the project. This uneven tension can be caused by insufficient counter-enamel, pressure, or misfit of the enamel on a firing trivet.

Cracks in second or successive coats

Cracks that appear in the second coat of enamel, or successive coats (enamel over enamel), may be identified as one of the following.

1. Broken Star Cracks. These cracks occur when the counter-enamel has burned away in one area, but not all over.

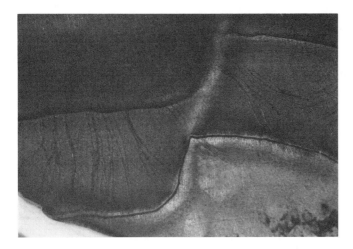

Fig. 13-9 *Straight cracks, caused by uneven tension.*

2. Cloisonné Wire Cracks. Cracks at the end of a cloisonné wire occur due to the expansion of silver being greater than the copper or the enamel.

3. Parallel Cracks. Cracks which run across the piece parallel to the metal are caused by the firing of two mismatched enamels with different expansion rates.

4. Straight Line Cracks. Cracks which appear in a perfect surface upon refiring are due to improper cooling, incorrectly weighting down the fired enamel, or because of heavy heat drain from the firing assemblage. This type of crack can also be caused by removing the project from the kiln before the enamels have fused to each other after the initial shock of being placed into the heat.

5. Cracks in Opaque Surfaces. Cracks which appear in an opaque surface only, while none show in the transparents, may be caused by the opaque enamel being pickled. The pickle will attack lead-bearing opaques.

6. Limoges Cracks. When newly applied painting enamel is fired before it is completely dry, cracks will appear in the Limoges areas. Painting enamel applied too thickly will also produce cracks in Limoges work.

SOLUTIONS: Try to maintain a good even coat of enamel at all times. If the enamel surface on which you are working is thick, apply another coat of counter-enamel to help balance the tension. Always counter-enamel the project for greater stability of the surfaces. Cool slowly in a draft-free environment. Do not take a warm enamel into a cold atmosphere for several hours. Always weight and shape the enameled form before it cools below 1000°F (538°C). An enamel project is most workable between 1500°F (816°C) and 1000°F (538°C). Below these temperatures, it will usually crack if pressure is applied. Unfired enamels that have been transported during the cold winter months must be warmed to room temperature before firing.

Ghost cracks

After refiring a cracked enamel, fine crack lines may still remain visible although the enamel has healed. These ghost lines are caused by either oxidation of the metal under the cracked glass surface because it was not repaired immediately, or exposure to water or pickle which has seeped into the crack.

The solution to this problem is to refire the cracked enamel immediately without exposing it to any liquids.

Cracks in old enamel surfaces

The repair of cracks in old enamels that have been abused during their lifetime is a restoration procedure requiring special skills beyond the scope of this book. See Further Reading for useful books on this subject.

Bubbles trapped in transparent surfaces

DEFECT: On occasion, you will observe hundreds of minute pinpoint bubbles seemingly trapped within a transparent enamel surface after firing. This tends to give the transparents an undesirable opacity.

SOLUTION: Use no binder at all while applying the enamels or, alternatively, dilute the binder to reduce the concentration of organic matter present. Successive firings also help to "clear" the transparent enamel once this characteristic has been observed. Each coat should be fired to total transparency before a successive coat is applied.

Opaques turning transparent

DEFECT: On occasion, you may fire an opaque and upon removal from the kiln, find it is transparent. This is the natural characteristic of an arsenic-opacified opaque enamel that has been fired at a higher temperature than recommended. When these opaques are fired at extreme heat (above 1650°F [898°C]) the temperature of the opacifier is exceeded. This causes transparency to develop.

SOLUTION: Refire the enamel at the regular 1500°F (816°C) temperature. The opaque enamel that had become transparent will return to its opaque state.

Fig. 13-10 *Cloisonné burn out, caused by overfiring or creation of a eutectic reaction in the kiln.*

Cloisonné burnout

DEFECT: The most dire enameling problem is when—after many hours of preparation—you remove a precious piece from the kiln to find the fine silver cloisons in a puddle on the metal surface. The cause of the cloisons melting is overfiring, firing at too high a temperature (beyond the melting point of the fine silver, 1761°F [969°C]), or a eutectic has been created between the pure copper and pure silver. Eutectic is the melting-flowing point of the two metals, which is a temperature much lower than that possible if the metals were heated separately. In the presence of a flux (in this case, enamel) this eutectic action can take place at 1425°F (774°C).

If a wire lies unevenly on the enamel surface, the point where it rests will sink deeper into the supporting coat of enamel. With successive firings, the wire can sink just deep enough to touch the copper. Once this happens, a temperature of 1425°F (774°C) will cause the silver to melt in combination with the copper. Even the most experienced enamelist has experienced this dilemma and, throughout your enameling career, it will probably happen more than once.

Many a "jewel" has been created from this traumatic experience. The best approach here is to forget about it for a couple of days and then consider it for an experimental technique. Approach this enamel's "cure" with an open mind, experiment and enjoy what can happen.

Fire the enamel at an equally high temperature again, let it cool and observe its characteristics. Clean the edges and fire again, adding enamel to any bare areas, perhaps different colors overlaid to produce jewellike effects. Vary the temperature and enjoy the wonderful possibilities: fire the piece at an angle so the colors will run one into the other (not long enough for the enamel to run off the edge); change the angle and refire; add more cloisons; add lumps and threads. Enjoy the heat and the media; wonderful, spontaneous results are yours for the taking and it may be the most interesting enamel you ever make.

Removing enamel from a metal surface

The time may arise when none of the aforementioned solutions give satisfactory results. Do not throw the piece away; the metal is still usable and the enamel can be removed if you so wish.

There are three easy methods to remove the enamel from a metal surface:

1. Place the enamel on a trivet assemblage and fire in the kiln for 2 to 3 minutes. Remove the assemblage from the kiln, pick up the enamel with a pair of tongs and plunge the red-hot enamel piece into a bucket of cold water. Thermal shock will remove quantities of the enamel from the metal surface. This process may be repeated until the surface is completely bare. Any glass residue left on the metal can be removed by stoning, filing or with a heatless grinder on a flex-shaft tool.

2. Pounding the enamel form with a wooden mallet on a steel stake or plate will cause the enamel to shatter and fall off. Care must be taken during this process: protect your eyes with glasses, as the flying enamel is a potential projectile. Remove the shattered glass from around the work area as it falls from the metal. The pieces of glass can become embedded in the tools, leaving ugly marks that will have to be dealt with later. The embedded glass can also damage the surfaces of the tools, including steel. Any glass residue left on the metal can be removed by stoning, filing, or with a heatless grinder on a flex-shaft tool.

3. When the base metal is silver or gold, it is less frustrating and easier to put the offending metal with the rest of your scraps. The enamel will act as a flux when the time comes to melt down the scrap metal. Alternatively, it is acceptable to return it to the foundry with the rest of your scraps for refining.

PART FOUR

A ready reference to
26 enameling techniques

Fig. IV-1   Bare Branches. *Kay Johnson. Basse-taille, transparent enamels on copper; 7" diameter.*

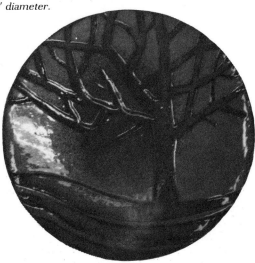

Overleaf: Second Skins, *1981. Martha Banyas. Wallpiece, cloisonné, underglaze pencils and basse-taille on copper with feathers; 8" × 8" × 2". Photograph, the artist.*

Basse-taille

Basse-taille, a French word meaning "low cut," literally describes this style of enameling. The technique dates to Renaissance Europe; truly fine examples of basse-taille are on display in art museums.

The surface of the metal is disturbed (textured) in some way from its original plane and transparent enamels are applied over the complete surface. Light is reflected as it hits the metal, and shines back through the transparents creating illusionary depths and chatoyancy.

Basse-taille can be executed on any of the metals used for enameling; silver gives this technique an added dimension and the luminosity achieved is worthy of the metal.

Textures for basse-taille are achieved using silversmithing techniques; the most suitable are engraving, chiseling and carving, stamping, etching, repoussé and chasing, and combinations of the above. When the desired texture has been achieved, several thin layers of transparent enamels are fired over the entire metal surface.

Fig. IV-2 Death and the Man, *detail, 1964. Mel Someroski. Basse-taille; roundel 10" diameter. Photograph, the artist.*

Fig. IV-3 *Convex panel, 1980. June Schwarcz. Basse-taille, etched and electroplated; transparent enamels; 11" × 7⅞". Photograph, the artist.*

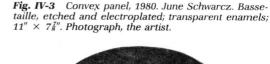

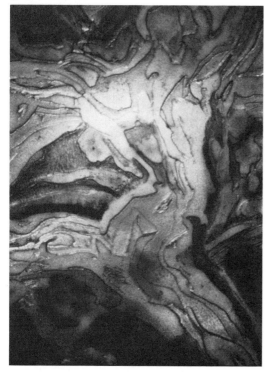

Camaïeu

A form of Limoges, Camaïeu has been associated with the great grisaille and Limoges painters of the Sixteenth Century. Camaïeu differs from grisaille in that finely ground white opaques are applied over transparents, rather than over the black background of grisaille.

The background transparent is fired onto the metal surface in the usual manner. Finely ground (325–400 mesh) white enamel is steeped in a mixture of distilled water and one or two drops of binder (Klyr-Fire or a similar binder). Alternatively, the painting enamel can be mixed with an oil.

Using an #000 sable-hair brush, a very thin application of white enamel is painted onto the transparent and fired. Adding many thin coats, the white enamel is built up in the traditional manner. Subtle colors other than white can be added to the design.

Fig. IV-4 Beloved Pan. *Margaret Seeler. Camaïeu on copper; 2" × 2½". In the collection of The Wichita Art Association, Inc.*

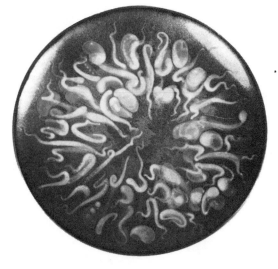

Fig. IV-5 Bean Spring Sprouts. *Harold B. Helwig. Camaïeu, white over transparent green enamel on copper; 10.8cm diameter. Photograph, the artist.*

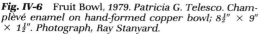

Fig. IV-6 Fruit Bowl, 1979. Patricia G. Telesco. Champlèvé enamel on hand-formed copper bowl; 8½" × 9" × 1½". Photograph, Ray Stanyard.

Fig. IV-7 My Mother's Eyes. Bowl. *Patricia G. Telesco. Champlèvé enamel on hand-formed copper bowl; 8" × 7" × 2". Photograph, Ray Stanyard.*

Champlèvé

Champlèvé is a style of enameling similar to basse-taille, but differing in the method of enamel application. Craftsmen of Medieval Europe were well acquainted with the champlèvé technique and many wonderful historical examples are available for your viewing pleasure. The method of preparing the metal for champlèvé in ancient times was by chiseling recessed areas and cavities into thick metal (16–14 gauge [1.299 mm–1.629 mm]) and filling these cavities with both transparent and opaque enamels. The thick metal edges or *raised planes* (translation of the French word *champlèvé*) were left without an enamel coating. This effect created bold lines with strong contrasts between the enamel and the metal.

Fig. IV-8 *Bracelet. Charlene Modena. Photoetched champlèvé enamel on copper; 3" high. Photograph, the artist.*

Today, the most common method of achieving the recessed cavities is by etching. Use 16–14 (1.290 mm–1.629 mm) gauge metal. Areas not to be etched must be protected with an acid-resistant coating. Asphaltum is a frequently used material, although other resists can be substituted, with excellent results. The metal project with its protective, acid-resistant coating is placed in strong acid (refer to a jewelry manual for etching instructions) and the unprotected areas are etched away to the desired depth.

Chiseling, repoussé, or chasing can also be used to create the recessed design in your metal. Or, a pierced sheet of metal soldered onto a backing plate of solid metal can be used to create a similar effect. When this technique is used, a solder with a high melting point is needed; with careful use, it should not reflow during the enameling process. The composition of the solder will promote pits in the enamel; consequently, it is advisable to remove any excess solder from the cavities before commencing the enameling processes.

Only the recessed areas are covered with enamels. Often the bare metal areas in champlèvé are gold plated for extra richness.

Fig. IV-10 The Sheep: Ascent to Heaven, *1981. Correen Kaufman. Pin, fine and sterling silver, cloisonné, plastic sheep cast and fabricated; 2½" × 3". Photograph, the artist.*

Fig. IV-9 Jonquils. *Bertie Wilson. Concave cloisonné on copper; transparent and opaque enamels; repoussé bulb. 8" × 10".*

Fig. IV-11 Mildred Pierce, *1982. Barbara Satterfield. Pin, silver cloisonné on copper, sterling silver setting; 3" × 2½". Photograph, the artist.*

Cloisonné

Most well-known of all the enameling techniques, cloisonné has almost become a household word. However, the term is widely misused and you may find it applied to inexpensive costume jewelry made from plastic with painted metallic lines, machine-stamped trinkets, or mass-produced champlevé.

The term cloisonné comes from the French word, *cloison*, meaning an enclosed area or cell. The three styles of cloisonné most often seen are: concave, convex, and flat. Each type is executed in the same manner; only the finishing techniques separate them into the individual categories.

Concave cloisonné: Each cell has less enamel in its center than around the cloisonné wire, giving a concave appearance. Capillary attraction during firing achieves this effect.

Convex cloisonné: The enamel in each cell is fired so that it forms slightly rounded mounds—or cushions—above the cloisonné wires to give a sculptural feeling.

Flat cloisonné; This is the most popular type of cloisonné. Flat cloisonné enamels are fired and stoned so that the enamel and the wires all share the same common level. After stoning, the surface can be finished in three ways:

1. Matt finish is often seen on enamels from the German schools. After the stoning process, the surface is wet-and-dry papered to a smooth satin finish. A final coat of paste wax protects the finish.

2. Semigloss finishes to cloisonné enamels can be produced by refining the stoned surface with various grades of grinding and polishing compounds on a lapidary wheel. The techniques are similar to those used for polishing cabochon stones.

3. Glossy cloisonné surfaces are acquired by a quick "flash firing" after the final stoning has taken place. Alternatively, the stoned enamel can be polished on a lapidary wheel with grinding and polishing compounds to a full gloss finish.

Complete step-by-step instructions for the cloisonné technique can be found in Chapter 10.

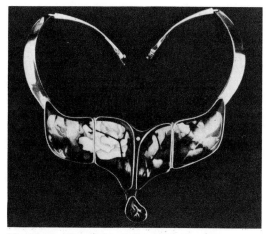

Fig. IV-12   Ghost Rose Collar, *1981. Merry Lee Howell and John Howell. Cloisonné enamels, sterling, 18K gold, diamond, and garnet; setting forged and fabricated; 8" wide. Photograph, Trini Contreras.*

Fig. IV-13   *Untitled pin. Thomas J. Terceira. Copper cloisonné on copper; carved delrin; 2¼" × 5". Photograph, Anthony C. Terceira.*

Decal application

Ceramic decals available from pottery supply stores can be incorporated into an enamel project quite successfully. Large and small compositions of birds, flowers, fruit, and initials are among the motifs available. The decals are made by a printing process—usually lithoprint or silkscreen—using ceramic stains and metallic oxides for the imagery. These designs are often trite, but taken out of context or cut into sections and incorporated into an enamel project, the decals can add another dimension. Decals may be used on the final enamel surface or between layers of transparents.

Soak the decal in warm water according to the directions and slip the backing sheet off the imagery onto the enamel surface. Do not turn the decal over. Remove all excess water from the decal, then, use a blotter, linen cloth, or a piece of felt to squeegee out all wrinkles and air bubbles. Dry thoroughly; overnight drying is recommended. Place the enamel, with the applied decal now totally devoid of all moisture, into the kiln or an oven at 350°F–400°F (177°C–205°C) to burn out the transfer paper (the decal will take on an ugly brown appearance). Place the project into a regular kiln and fire at normal firing temperature until you observe a gloss surface (approximately $1\frac{1}{2}$ minutes at 1450°F (788°C). Check for total surface gloss. Fire 30 seconds longer if necessary.

It is necessary to preheat the decal/enamel composition at the lower temperature to burn out all the organic material (transfer paper) before the regular firing. Do not try to accomplish the organic burn-out and the maturation of the decal on the enamel surface at the same time; bubble lines occur when the initial thermal shock lines burn into crack lines. There is no remedy for this problem once it occurs.

Add to the decal imagery by wet packing or Limoges techniques, or overcoat with transparents. Experiment, and enjoy this alternative imagery maker.

Fig. IV-14 *Dress-up doll necklace, 1982. June Jasen. Silver cloisonné enamel on copper; doll, $4\frac{5}{8}$" high. Photograph, Lex Tice.*

Fig. IV-15 *Dress-up doll necklace. June Jasen. Silver cloisonné enamel integrated with low-fire ceramic materials. Photograph, Lex Tice.*

Fig. IV-16 Another Season, 1982. Collaboration: Enamel, Laura K. Popenoe; Beads, Martin and Lucia. Electroformed cloisonné enamel; pendant, 3″ × 4½″. Photograph, Elia Haworth.

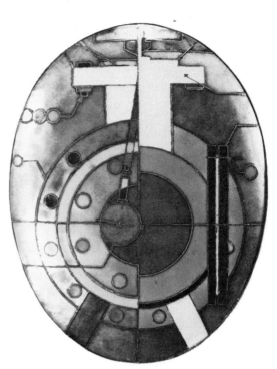

Fig. IV-17 Slac Panel III, 1981. June Schwarcz. Electroformed enamel; 13¼″ × 10⅜″ × 2⁷⁄₁₆″. Photograph, the artist.

Electroforming and enameling

Electroforming is the electrical deposition of a thick metal coating onto a base. The base can either be a temporary matrix or a permanent surface.

With electroforming, it is possible to create textural surfaces and divisions for enameling techniques such as cloisonné, champlèvé, basse-taille, or plique-à-jour. The metal can be enameled first and then electroformed; vice versa; or a combination of the two as the art form develops. When the enamel is to be exposed to the electroforming bath and chemicals, use only *acid-resistant* enamels.

Firescale/Scalex designing

The firescale which forms on copper may provide an excellent design background for transparents. The organic patterns are spontaneous and often quite pleasing. Discarded Scalex flakes are also usable.

The black and red oxides that develop as firescale are useful designing tools. Heat the bare copper to annealing temperature and allow to cool. Keep this piece of copper away from your worktable, other enamels and other workers. When cool, dust off any loose flakes and observe the surface. If you like what you see, proceed. If you do not like what you see, pickle the copper and start again.

Effective designs can often be executed when only part of a surface is enameled, allowing firescale to develop in the unenameled areas; e.g., enamel the sky and let a mountain range develop from the firescale deposits. Good utilization of these deposits will develop with experimentation.

When the firescale imagery is to your innovative liking, apply transparent enamel and fire. Successive coats of enamel can be added until the desired results are achieved.

Fired Scalex (the firescale inhibitor that flakes off bare copper after the metal has been taken from the kiln) and flakes of firescale are also usable. The flakes can be fused between coats of transparents, in a similar application to foils, to obtain shadows and organic patterning. Experiment, and enjoy the results of spontaneity.

Fig. IV-19 Untitled panel. Fred Uhl Ball. Copper with clear liquid flux, folded to create seaming; assembled on a wooden frame; 4' × 5' × 2". Photograph, Kurt Fishback. In the collection of the Office of the President, Weinstock's Department Store, Sacramento, California.

Fig. IV-18 Emerging Planet, 1982. Pamela Carey Steele. Painting with liquid enamels, and use of firescale; 15" × 15". Photograph, the artist.

Fig. IV-20 *Brooch. Belle and Roger Kuhn. Transparent enamels on fine silver, textured foil; sterling silver setting with reticulation; $1\frac{3}{4}''$ × $2''$. Photograph, the artists.*

Foils

Gold and silver foils, pure metal in thin sheets, can be fired into an enamel to add luster to transparents. When copper or silver is selected as the base for the enamel project, foils add a luxurious quality. The enamelist's foil should not be confused with gold or silver leaf. The foil is best purchased from an enamel supplier who knows its intended use. While some gold and silver leaf can be used, it is so extremely thin that, without careful monitoring, it will burn away during the firings. There are also leaf substitutes available; avoid these, as they will fire to a dark soot deposit and ruin the enamel surface.

Foils can be fired onto the final surface, used between layers of enamel, or added either before or after cloisons have been laid. As long as there is an enamel surface to which the foil can adhere during the firing process, anything is possible. When foil is applied to large areas, it should be broken into smaller sections rather than applied as one continuous sheet. When handling foil, keep it between the sheets of tissue in which it is sold, or between sheets of tracing paper. Do not let your skin come in contact with the metal, as body oils contaminate the foil. Cut the foil designs through the protective paper with small sharp scissors or with an X-acto knife. Pick up the design with a slightly dampened paintbrush and position carefully. No binder is necessary; a little water around the edges will hold the foil in place.

Tradition dictates that foil should be pricked completely to allow trapped gases to escape during the firing process. Recent tests show that this is not necessary and it is busywork that we can well do without. The foil does have to be completely dry before firing. When time permits, overnight drying is recommended.

Fire the foil onto the enamel surface at 1450°F (788°C) for a scant $1\frac{1}{2}$ minutes; check for proper adhesion. Fire for 30 seconds longer if necessary. Additional coats of enamel may be fired over the foil.

Fumed enamels

The magical iridescence of rainbow colors as they play across a glass surface is irresistible. The long tradition of fuming has belonged to glassblowers; during the Art Nouveau era, artists used fuming techniques to perfection—Tiffany glass being the premier example.

Unfortunately, fuming requires a process which is very dangerous to one's health. Tin chloride ($SnCl_2$), the chemical required for fuming, can cause heavy metal poisoning if inhaled or taken internally. Iron chloride ($FeCl_2$) and gold chloride ($AuCl_3$) can also be used for fuming; each chemical will achieve slightly different effects. These chemicals are applied when the enamel is taken from the kiln.

If you must pursue this decorative finish for enamels, use an extremely well-ventilated area, preferably with a good exhaust fan, and wear protective clothing. Read all the literature available on these chemicals and observe all warnings and instructions; proceed with the utmost caution.

Fig. IV-21 Venus. *Harold B. Helwig. Grisaille, fumed enamels on copper; 29cm. Photograph, the artist.*

Fig. IV-22 Moth, 1980. John Paul Miller. 18K gold granulation with transparent enamels on pure gold; $2\frac{3}{4}''$ × 3". Photograph, the artist.

Fig. IV-23 Ode to Red Shoes, 1980. Barbara Mail. Pin with detachable pin stem; 24K cloisonné on sterling silver, 14K gold, carved ivory, green tourmaline; enameled, cast, constructed, carved; $2\frac{1}{4}''$ × 1" × $\frac{1}{2}''$. In the collection of Marilyn Cooper. Photograph, the artist.

Gold granulation and enameling

Granulation, a most delicate and decorative metal technique, is the process of eutectically fusing two metals together without solder. Gold-smiths of the ancient Mediterranean area were the ultimate masters of granulation. Small grains or granules of gold were fused to a backing sheet of gold in intricate designs of flowers, foliage, and linear abstractions. Hundreds of exciting examples are preserved in art museums. No solder is used in the granulation process; therefore, this technique is ideal for enameling.

The best metals to use are 24-karat gold and high-karat gold alloys, although fine silver will work in a similar manner. The granules can be arranged and fused onto the backing plate to simulate a type of cloison, or used purely for decorative purposes.

A granulation effect can also be achieved by firing small granules of metal onto an existing enamel surface (Fig. III-23). This alternative is an excellent way to use up scraps of cloisonné wire (24-karat gold or fine silver). When a small section of wire is placed on a charcoal block and heated with a torch, the metal will naturally form spherical balls as it melts. These granules can be applied at the same time and by the same method used for cloisonné wire.

Fig. IV-24 Philadelphia Fat Cats. *D. X. Ross. Brooch, grisaille enamels with turquoise; sterling silver setting with 14K gold accents; 2" wide. Photograph, Elin Dickens.*

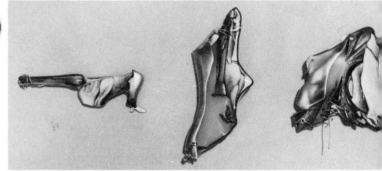

Fig. IV-25 The Boarder I, II and III. *Mary Ann Papenek-Miller. Three pins, grisaille enamels on copper; carving, Plexiglas, electroformed sterling silver. Photograph, the artist.*

Grisaille

Another French word for our enameling vocabulary, grisaille is derived from *gris*, meaning "gray". Many descriptive enameling terms are French, because France was the ultimate enameling center for such a long period in our recent history. The great French enamel painters from the area of Limoges set the standards and the terminology for the art of enameling.

A grisaille enamel is most often seen with a black background over which many thin layers of white have been added. Fired after each application, the enamel is built up to produce all the shades of gray, from black through white.

The finely ground (325–400 mesh) white enamel is steeped in either a distilled water and binder mixture, or a selected oil, and then applied with a fine sable-hair brush in very thin coats, firing after each application. If the fired white enamel cracks or pulls apart, it is a sign that the finely ground enamel application was too thick for the particle size. A mistake of this nature may be rectified by stoning and adding a further thin coat of white.

Pastel transparents, lusters and other subtle additives can be incorporated into the final firing. Fuming is a wonderful addition: the iridescence brings the black background alive, shimmering with a rainbow of subtle colors.

Impasto

A term borrowed from the painters, *impasto* is the laying on of finely ground (325–400 mesh) painting enamel. Unlike grisaille and Camaïeu, the impasto is applied to a bare metal surface. Because there is no other enamel present, the painting enamel can be built up into a relief upon the metal surface without the fear of cracking after firing. Impasto can be modeled into sculptural detail, giving an impression of significant three-dimensionality.

The acid-resistant painting enamel is steeped in distilled water to which one or two drops of adhesive binder have been added. It is then applied to the clean metal surface with a #000 sable-hair brush. Keep the working area damp. Once the applied enamel has dried, it is quite difficult to add further enamel. What you see while the enamel is still wet is what you will achieve after the firing. (The dried enamel looks much more opaque than the fired enamel.)

Fire the painting enamel on bare copper at 1450°F (788°C) for a scant 75 seconds. Mere seconds too long in the kiln will produce burn-out. When the enamel is cool, clean and apply one coat of transparent in selected color. After the transparent has been fired, additional thin coats of white painting enamel may be added to the design. After the initial transparent firing, the painting enamel must be applied in thin applications, as described for grisaille. Additional coats of transparent enamel may also be added. This process works only with acid-resistant enamels.

Fig. IV-26 Warm Sea Friend. *Harold B. Helwig. Impasto and Limoges with metallic oxides; pure gold and pure platinum details; 15.2cm diameter. Photograph, the artist.*

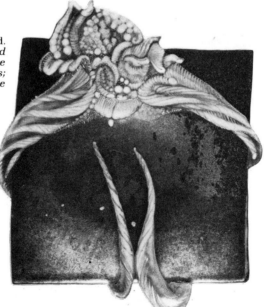

Limoges

In the latter part of the Fifteenth Century, Limoges, a small town in Southern France, became known for a new technique in enameling. This technique adopted the name of the town, and it is this name we still use to describe painting techniques in enameling.

Using painting grade enamels (325 and finer mesh), thin coats are built up on the background enamel. Each thin coat must be fired after application. Too thick a coating of the painting enamel may produce separations (fineline cracks) after the enamel has been fired.

The painting enamel is steeped in a binder (Klyr-Fire or similar) and distilled water mixture or an oil such as oil of lavender or oil of clove, for application with fine quality brushes. The water-based painting enamels and the oil-based painting enamels will produce distinctive variations.

Step-by-step instructions for mixing painting enamels and using the Limoges technique are detailed in Chapter 8.

Fig. IV-27 Woman—Eternal as the Sea, 1981. Barbara Satterfield. Limoges enamel on copper, sterling silver setting, walnut; 1¼" × 2". Photograph, the artist.

Fig. IV-28 Merlin's Vestment. Collaboration: Enamel, Laura K. Popenoe; Beadwork, Martin and Lucia. Limoges enamel with gold and silver inlays, electroplated; 2" × 4½", 18" tassels. Photograph, Art Rogers.

Liquid and crackle enamels

Liquid and crackle enamels are enamel ground to a fine particle size and suspended in fluid. Liquid enamels are often used in industry for spray application. For decorative art purposes, a surface that has been previously enameled can be overcoated with a liquid enamel by dipping, brushing, or spraying. Sgraffito work through dried liquid enamel will produce satisfying results. Sprayed liquid enamel may be used as an alternative to dusting when applying stencils. Commercially available liquid and crackle enamels may contain different product compositions.

Spontaneous surface designs can be achieved by applying liquid enamel over a previously fired surface, drying and firing at the normal temperature. When the liquid enamel is not disturbed (scratched through), it will pull apart during firing to expose the enamel surface underneath. This process is described as crackle enamel, because of its cracked and crazed appearance. Crackle effect will not usually occur on small flat surfaces.

Fig. IV-29 *November Wader II, 1982. John Killmaster. Liquid enamels, sgraffito/grisaille on steel; hammered relief, black and white with transparents; 18" × 29". Photograph, H. Huff.*

Fig. IV-30 *Junction, 1982. Pamela Carey Steele. Wallpiece, painting techniques with liquid enamel on copper sections; 20" × 28". Photograph, the artist.*

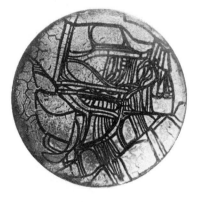

Fig. IV-31 Endless Homage, 1979. Jo Ann Tanzer. Liquid enamels on copper; sgraffito and crackle effects; 8" diameter. Photograph, the artist.

Fig. IV-32 Harvest Moon. *Duncan Berry. Mask; cloisonné; transparents and opaques over copper with lusters; sterling finial, hardwood handle 8" × 24". Photograph, the artist.*

Lusters and liquid gold, palladium, silver

When an enamel has undergone its many stages of preparation, firing, and refining, it may still need an extra "zap" to make it special. Lusters and liquid metals that are generally used by potters and in the ceramic industry may fill this occasional need. Since most basic ceramic glazes are made from compositions similar to that of glass and/or enamel, it is not unreasonable for the enamelist to borrow these materials from the ceramist.

Lusters add opalescence and mother-of-pearl finishes to an enamel surface (see color section). Experimentation and adaptation are wonderful tools, but do not use the lusters as a crutch to disguise uninspired enamels.

Liquid metals—gold, platinum, palladium, silver, etc.—can be applied by brush or pen, dried thoroughly, and fired to 1450°F (788°C) for a minute or so. Upon cooling, the metals need to be burnished with a glass brush for extra sparkle.

Metallic oxides

Pure oxides (pigments of the earth), such as black iron oxide, red iron oxide, and copper oxide, can be mixed with water and used in a manner similar to watercolors. Oxides bring a new dimension to the "paintability" of an enamel artist (see color section).

These oxides or stains are available in powder form. When suspended in a little water, the oxides can be flowed upon an enamel surface to produce innovative results. Oxides may be applied over the first coat of opaque enamel to add dimension and color. If used over foils (after a transparent enamel coat), the oxides will produce subtle colors and definition.

The only rule for using oxides is that the pigment has to have either a recipient coat of enamel into which it will be absorbed, or a transparent coat applied over the oxide to seal it in. These metallic oxides are not vitreous, but will color an enameled surface when fired.

Fig. IV-33 Black Forest, 1982. Pamela Carey Steele. Metallic oxides and enamel on steel; Watercolor painting technique; 10″ × 10″. Photograph, the artist.

Fig. IV-34 Ceylon Fish, detail, 1974. Mel Some- roski. Plique-à-jour; 4". Photograph, the artist.

Fig. IV-35 Oranges Bowl, 1978. Kathleen M. Farling. Plique-à-jour, cloisonné/acid method; 2" × 4" × 4". Photo- graph, courtesy of Cin- cinnati Museum Photo- graphic Services.

Fig. IV-36 Hot Air Bal- loon, 1978. Kathleen M. Farling. Plique-à-jour, pierced method; 4" × 2½". Photograph, the artist.

Plique-à-jour

Even without knowing the translation, a name like plique-à-jour, con- jures up wonderful imagery. Plique-à-jour literally translates as "light of day"—an apt description of these beautiful enamels.

Plique-à-jour allows the passage of light through the enamel. Be- cause there is no backing metal, there is nothing to absorb or reflect the light. This results in a delicate stained-glass effect, with jewel like transparent enamel areas contrasting against the metal.

A plique-à-jour enamel requires many painstaking hours to com- plete; patience and humility are your most important tools for this technique. As light is required to pass through the enamel, voids in the metal must be created for this purpose. The negative spaces can be pierced or drilled into the metal (Fig. IV-34), or a cloisonné-type enamel can be produced on a backing which, upon completion, is removed (Fig. IV-35). This backing can be removed either by etching, or by delaminating the host metal, peeling it away from the enameled cells.

Traditionally, small bowls, lamps and jewelry have been made by this fragile technique. Many new innovations are possible to observe the "light of day."

Raku enameling

Borrowed from the ceramic arts, raku is a firing tradition from the Japanese potteries. When a matured enamel is taken from the kiln, it is placed in a reducing atmosphere—a sealed container in which pine needles, sawdust, paper, or various other flammable materials have been deposited. The hot enamel causes combustion of the materials, thus creating the reduction atmosphere which lusters the enamel. As the combustible materials burn, oxygen in the container is used up, creating the reduction atmosphere.

Raku enameling is an experimental technique. One may also add compatible ceramic raku glazes to the enamel surface before firing to produce variables.

Fig. IV-37 *Raku enamel, 1982. David Berfield. Raku glaze on roofing copper with liquid enamels; 34" × 36". Photograph, Mary Randlett.*

Fig. IV-38 *Raku wall panel, 1981. RoseAnna Tendler Worth. Raku on copper with copper foil sculptural element; 17" diameter. Photograph, the artist.*

Fig. IV-39   *Detail of marble effect achieved through the scrolling technique.*

Scrolling, swirling, trailing

Usually considered "hobby" techniques, scrolling, swirling and trailing—approached with an open mind and an aesthetic viewpoint—can add to the enamelist's repertoire.

Scrolling, swirling and trailing all describe basically the same technique. Lump and thread enamel is fired onto an already enameled surface. While the project is still in the kiln, you can upset the order or arrangement of the lumps and threads by pulling a scrolling tool through the molten enamels. Take care to wear a heat-resistant glove, flame retardant clothes and special safety glasses, as you will be working directly inside the kiln, exposed to at least 1500°F (816°C) temperatures. The object to be scrolled must be firmly secured, or working the tool through the enamel could pull the project off its trivet.

Many exciting effects can be achieved as you pull the tool through the molten enamel. Several different colored threads, pulled one way and then another, will produce moiré patterns. Lumps arranged and then pulled into feathered patterns can produce marbleization not unlike the marbled endpapers of hand-bound books. The possibilities are endless.

Separation enamel

Separation enamel can be applied to an enamel surface to produce pleasing abstract designs. When fired, the separation enamel causes the previously enameled surfaces to slip and separate, creating patterns. This technique is especially appropriate for steep-sided vessels.

Two or three contrasting colors of enamel should first be fired onto the metal surface. Use a combination of soft-fusing and medium-fusing enamels for best results. A good, thick counter enamel (two coats) is also recommended, because the separation enamel will be fired at much higher temperatures than usual.

Apply the liquid separation enamel in a series of geometric patterns: dots, dashes, stripes, wavy lines, etc. Some of the pattern should be carried onto the top of the bowl or container. Separation enamels must be thoroughly dry before firing.

Fire in the kiln for 2 to 3 minutes at 1650°F (898°C). The intense heat combined with the separation enamel will cause the enamel to separate along the pattern lines, exposing the undercoats of enamel. Many pleasing patterns can be produced with this method and, with a little experience, unusual decorative enamels will be produced.

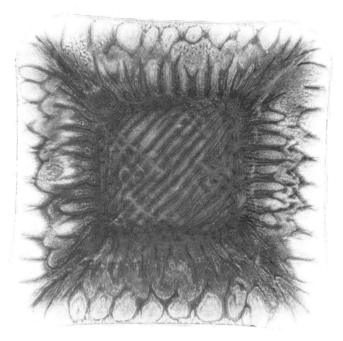

Fig. IV-40 *Separation bowl. Eileen Maxon. Transparent enamels on copper, separation enamels; 5" × 5". Photograph, F. Bruce Maxon.*

Sgraffito

Sgraffito, meaning to scribe or scratch, is an apt name for this enameling technique. Using a sharp object (scribe, toothpick or any suitable probe), linear patterns are drawn through the unfired enamel to the bare metal or previously enameled surface.

Before the sgraffito is fired, all extraneous particles of enamel must be removed from the scribed design. Use a slightly dampened fine paintbrush to manipulate the stray granules. After the sgraffito design has been fired, additional enamels may be added, according to the dictates of your design. Step-by-step instructions for a sgraffito project are given in Chapter 5.

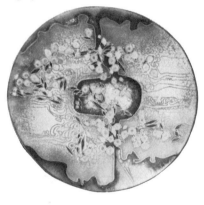

Fig. IV-42 Tray. Margaret Fischer. Sgraffito and cloisonné on copper; 6" diameter. Photograph, the artist.

Fig. IV-41 Composition with Nudes and Sunflowers, 1982. John Killmaster. Sgraffito/grisaille enamels on hammered steel with small areas of transparents; 35" × 35". Photograph, H. Huff.

Stencils

A quick and easy method of applying designs to an enamel surface, stencils are particularly suitable for production techniques. Stenciling is often combined with sgraffito.

The stencil can be cut from a variety of materials. For limited use, strong paper will usually suffice. Different stenciling effects can be made by:

1. cutting a negative stencil that will produce a positive image;

2. cutting a positive stencil that will produce a negative image;

3. using found objects as stencils; e.g., leaves, ferns, grasses, etc.

A soft edge can be produced by elevating the stencil a few inches from the surface and dusting. A hard edge is achieved by placing the stencil directly onto the metal surface and clearing any extraneous enamel particles from the design before firing. Complete step-by-step directions for this technique are given in Chapter 5.

Fig. IV-43 Abstract Human Forms in Action, 1980. David Berfield. Stencil enamels on steel; 11" × 36". Photograph, copyright © 1980 Mary Randlett.

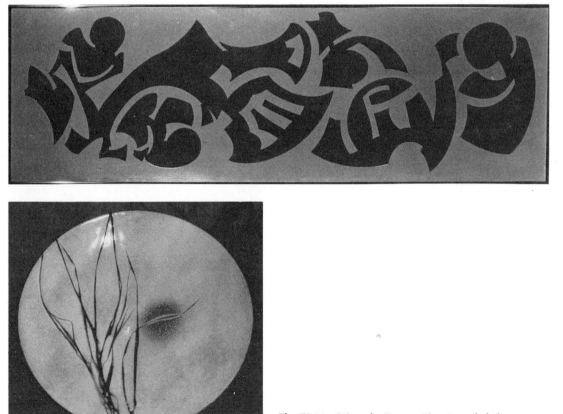

Fig. IV-44 Orientale. Roxane Riva. Stenciled plate, using found objects, leaves, ferns, etc.; enamel on copper; 8" diameter. Photograph, the artist.

Silkscreen enamels

Silkscreen enamels use similar processes to those used for silkscreen printing and serigraphy. An image is transferred onto fine silk held in a frame. The image can be applied by hand or by photographic processes. Special lacquers, photo-resist emulsions, or other resists are used to apply the imagery, which then becomes a positive/negative stencil. The resist, when applied to the silk in the desired pattern, blocks the open weave of the material. This masking will inhibit enamel (or ink, in the case of a serigraph) from passing through the silk in the areas that have been blocked.

Three different techniques can be used to apply enamel through the silk screen to the previously enameled surface.

Dry enamel screening

Examples are shown in Figures IV-44 and IV-45. Using silk of the appropriate size weave, 80-mesh enamel can be successfully dry-screened through the silk. A stiff card is used to draw the dry enamel over the silkscreen image. The great advantage to this method of applying the enamel is that no binders or oils are used, making multiple firings possible.

Fig. IV-46 Brooch. *Correen Kaufmann. Photo silkscreen, dry sifted enamels; copper and brass. Photograph, the artist.*

Fig. IV-45 Apple Head. *Peggy Hitchcock. Photo silkscreen enamels on steel plate; 12" × 12" × 1½". Photograph, the artist.*

Painting enamel screening

An example of this type of screening is shown in Figure IV-46. Painting grade enamel (325 mesh) can be used suspended in water and a small amount of binder (Klyr-Fire or similar). Using a traditional squeegee tool, the painting enamel is pushed through the silkscreen onto the enamel surface underneath.

Squeegee oil can be used instead of the water-based mixture. Careful and limited firing times and temperatures are needed when using the squeegee oil; overfiring can cause the imagery to disperse into the previously fired enamels.

Versa color screening

Versa Colors, marketed in small tubes, are overglaze decorating colors that can be applied using silkscreening techniques. As with the painting enamels, Versa Colors are pushed through the silk screen with a squeegee onto the previously enameled surface. It is advisable to fire a Versa Color surface only once. The Versa Color has similar firing characteristics to the painting enamels when suspended in squeegee oil.

Fig. IV-48 Yellow Brick Road, *1980. Cheryll Leo-Gwin. Photo silkscreen painting enamels on steel 10" × 8" × 1". Photograph, the artist.*

Fig. IV-47 The Catch, *1979. Jo Ann Tanzer. Silkscreen and stencils, dry sifted enamel on steel; 12" × 12". Photograph, the artist.*

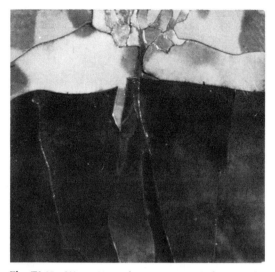

Fig. IV-49 Warm November. *Margaret Fischer. Torch-fired enamels on copper foil; 14" × 14". Photograph, the artist.*

Fig. IV-50 *Enamel beads. Betty Hearst. Transparent and opaque enamels on copper tubing; 1" long.*

Torch-fired enamels

It is possible to fire enamels onto a metal surface using a torch flame rather than firing the enamel in a kiln. The firing equipment could be an elaborate silversmithing torch using natural gas or acetylene gas-and-air combinations, or a simple propane torch. The flame is directed onto the *underside* of the metal, heating the enamel from below. The advantages of torch firing are that you can constantly watch the enamel mature and that the enamel project is not limited to any kiln size.

Three-dimensional enamel beads can be produced in a similar manner. A section of hollow copper rod is heated in the flame and dipped into the granular enamel. The rod is rotated in the torch flame to mature the enamel. Rotation aids heat dispersion and will prevent the enamel from slipping off the surface while in its molten state. Gestural swirling colors result from this rotation. Successive coats of enamel may be added to enhance the quality of the bead.

Underglazes and overglazes

Underglaze D

Underglaze D is a commercially available liquid for use under transparent enamels. It can be applied directly to bare copper in a linear design or it can be rubbed into recessed, etched surfaces to help highlight textures and patterns. When the underglaze is thoroughly dry, apply a sifted coat of the selected transparent color and fire at normal temperatures.

Fine line black

Fine Line Black is applied over fired enamels. Personal preference and the job at hand dictate the applicator—use either a fine paintbrush or a nib pen. When it has dried completely, the Fine Line Black is fired in the conventional manner. Fine Line Black can be used between layers of enamel, or on the final surface.

Ceramic underglazes

Underglaze pencils and crayons useful for detailing, shading and highlighting must be applied to matt enamel surfaces. These underglazes will not adhere to a high-gloss surface. An enamel surface may be

Fig. IV-51 *Enamel plaque. Barbara Gibbons. Fine-Line Black and wet inlay enamels on steel; 6" × 6". Photograph, McDonald.*

Fig. IV-52 The Coronation. *Peggy Hitchcock. Photo silkscreen enamels with Fine Line Black; 9" × 11" × 1½". Photograph, the artist.*

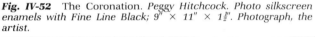

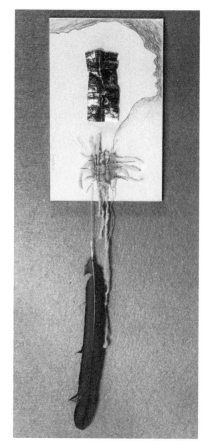

Fig. IV-54 Las Mesetas, *1982. John Killmaster. Limoges and silkscreen enamels on steel plate; 22" × 22". Photograph, the artist.*

Fig. *IV-55* Composition 27, *1981. JoAnne Vernon. Enamel on copper; ceramic overglazes and underglaze crayons; $15\frac{1}{2}" \times 9\frac{1}{2}" \times \frac{1}{2}"$. Photograph, the artist.*

made matt by stoning with an Alundum stone, sandblasting, or etching with matt salts. The underglaze colors are metallic oxides, not vitreous enamels, and will need either careful firing to incorporate them into the previously enameled surface, or should be overcoated with a clear flux or matt white.

Overglaze paints

Ceramic overglaze colors are available either in tubes (Versa Colors) or as palettes that can be moistened with oil or water. Overglaze colors should be applied only for the last firing; successive firings or too high a temperature may cause them to disperse into the enamel surface.

CAUTION: Do not overfire Underglaze D, Fine Line Black, or Versa Colors. Firing at 1450°F (788°C) for 75 seconds is sufficient.

Further Reading

Enameling

Ball, Fred Uhl, *Experimental Techniques in Enameling*. New York: Van Nostrand Reinhold, 1972.

Barsali, Isa Belli, *European Enamels*. London: The Hamlyn Publishing Group, Ltd., 1966.

Bates, Kenneth F., *Enameling: Principles and Practice*. The World Publishing Company, 1951; New York: Funk and Wagnalls paperback edition, 1974.

Bates, Kenneth F., *The Enamelist*. New York: Funk and Wagnalls paperback edition, 1975.

Harper, William, *Step-by-Step Enameling*. Racine, Wisconsin: Western Publishing Company.

Herbert, Maryon, *Metalwork and Enamelling*. New York: Dover Publications, Inc., 1971 (fourth edition).

Liban, Felicia, and Mitchell, Louise, *Cloisonné*. Radnor, Pennsylvania: Chilton Book Company, 1980.

Millenet, Louise-Ellie, *Enamelling on Metal*. London: The Technical Press, Ltd., 1951.

Rothenberg, Polly, *Metal Enameling*. New York: Crown Publishers, Inc., 1969.

Seeler, Margaret, *The Art of Enameling*. New York: Van Nostrand Reinhold, 1969, 1983.

Strosahl, J. Patrick, Judith Lull, and Coral Barnhart, *A Manual of Cloisonné and Champlevé Enameling*. New York: Charles Scribner's Sons, 1981.

Untracht, Oppi, *Enameling on Metal*. Radnor, Pennsylvania: Chilton Book Company, 1957.

Jewelry and silversmithing

Bovin, Murray, *Jewelry Making*. New York: Murray Bovin, 1952.

Choate, Sharr, and De May, Bonnie, *Creative Gold and Silversmithing*. New York: Crown Publishers, Inc., 1970.

Evans, Chuck, *Jewelry: Contemporary Design and Technique*. Worcester, Mass.: Davis Publications, 1983.

Finegold, Rupert, and Seitz, William, *Silversmithing*. Radnor, Pennsylvania: Chilton Book Company, 1983.

Loyen, Frances, *Silversmithing*. London: Thames and Hudson, Ltd., 1980.

McCreight, Tim, *The Complete Metalsmith*. Worcester, Mass.: Davis Publications, 1983.

Morton, Philip, *Contemporary Jewelry*. New York: Holt, Rinehart, and Winston, 1976 (second edition).

Steakley, Douglas, *Holloware Techniques*. New York: Watson Guptill Publications, 1979.

Untracht, Oppi, *Jewelry Concepts and Technology*. New York: Doubleday and Company, Inc., 1983.

Untracht, Oppi, *Metal Techniques for Craftsmen*. New York: Doubleday and Company, 1968.

Periodicals

Glass on Metal, a bimonthly newsletter published by the Ceramic Coating Company, Newport, Kentucky.

Art Hazards Newsletter, published by the Center for Occupational Hazards, Inc., New York, N.Y.

Metalsmith Magazine, published by The Society of North American Goldsmiths.

Index

Page numbers in **bold** refer to illustrations of enameling work